Spiritual Wisdom for Everyday People

Jamee Byrd Markert

Copyright © 2017 Jamee Byrd Markert

Revised August 2019
All rights reserved

ISBN-13: 9781537459370
ISBN-10: 1537459376
Library of Congress Control Number: 2016914944
CreateSpace Independent Publishing Platform
North Charleston, South Carolina

*I gratefully acknowledge the tremendously helpful
"Bible Hub" website: www.biblehub.com*

*Dedicated with all my love to Mom and Dad
Sara Byrd (1928–2015)
T. A. Byrd (1924–2015)*

Table of Contents

Acceptance and Tolerance	37
Asking God for Help	143
Challenges and Adversity	117
Choosing Positivity	32
Corrupt Leaders	124
Discerning Truth	98
Dissention and Anger	101
Encouragement	41
Esteem and Humility	28
Faith	63
Fear	108
Friendliness and Friendship	87
Forgiveness	60
Generosity	24
Gratitude	95
Guarding Your Thoughts and Words	52
Happiness	91
Helpfulness	46

Kindness and Compassion	19
Living on Earth	7
Love	85
Nature of God	138
On the Job	71
Parents and Parenting	66
Peace	50
Reaping What You Sow	104
Repentance and Redemption	133
Revenge	58
Sadness and Suffering	113
Things to Avoid	78
Trustworthiness and Integrity	75
Your Judgment Day	106
Your Relationship with God	126
Your Spiritual Journey	1
Worrying	111

Your Spiritual Journey

"You come from realms of unimaginable power and light, and you will return to those realms." *Terence McKenna*

"We are not human beings having a spiritual experience. We are spiritual beings having a human experience." *Pierre Teilhard de Chardin*

God created human beings with the hope that each of us would create wonderful things and contribute to the overall wellbeing of our world. He hopes we will choose to do good.

"We have a soul beneath the surface of the self. This soul forms the very core of our being and connects us to other souls and to a Higher power. Activation of this core point within is what allows us to transcend our baser nature and become a force for good in the world." *Mendel Kalmenson*

"We waste our lives when we do not pray and think and dream and plan and work toward magnifying God in all spheres of life." *John Piper*

"The end of life is to be like God, and the soul following God will be like him." *Socrates*

Earth is a training ground. "God loves you just the way you are, but He refuses to leave you that way." *Max Lucado*

"[L]et us throw off everything that hinders and the sin that so easily entangles, and let us run with perseverance the race marked out for us." *Hebrews 12:1*

Since you're a soul attending school here on Earth, you're continually being taught and tested throughout the day. The more spiritually advanced you become, the more challenging your lessons will become.

"Life is a succession of lessons which must be lived to be understood." *Ralph Waldo Emerson*

"We don't receive wisdom; we must discover it for ourselves after a journey that no one can take for us or spare us." *Marcel Proust*

"After all, you can't learn new things if you cannot admit you're a work in progress. Be open to recognizing your own faults, so you can grow …." *Ilya Pozin*

"The wise know too well their weakness to assume infallibility; and he who knows most knows best how little he knows." *Thomas Jefferson*

"The mind of an enlightened human being is flexible and adaptable. The mind of the ignorant person is conditioned and fixed." *Ajahn Sumedho*

Your Spiritual Journey

"Every experience God gives us, every person He puts in our lives is the perfect preparation for the future that only He can see." *Corrie ten Boom*

"A number of years ago, I met a wise man who changed my life.... He said, 'Stop asking God to bless what you're doing. Get involved in what God is doing—because it's already blessed.'" *Bono*

"Sir, my concern is not whether God is on our side; my greatest concern is to be on God's side ...." *Abraham Lincoln*

"The purpose of your life is far greater than your own personal fulfillment, your peace of mind, or even your happiness." *Rick Warren*

"Trust to God to weave your little thread into the great web ...." *George MacDonald*

"The purpose of life is to find your gift. The work of life is to develop it. The meaning of life is to give your gift away." *David Viscott*

"So we are to use our different gifts in accordance with the grace that God has given us. If our gift is to speak God's message, we should do it according to the faith that we have; if it is to serve, we should serve; if it is to teach, we should teach; if it is to encourage others, we should do so." *Romans 12:6-8*

"The person born with a talent they are meant to use will find their greatest happiness in using it." *Goethe*

"I have just three things to teach: simplicity, patience, compassion. These three are your greatest treasures." *Lao Tzu*

"If you can cultivate the right attitude, your enemies are your best spiritual teachers because their presence provides you with the opportunity to enhance and develop tolerance, patience and understanding." *The Dalai Lama*

"The struggle of life is one of our greatest blessings.
It makes us patient, sensitive, and Godlike.
It teaches us that although the world is full of suffering,
it is also full of the overcoming of it." *Helen Keller*

"Let us not become weary of doing good, for in due season we will reap a harvest if we do not give up." *Galatians 6:9*

"We do not want you to become lazy, but to imitate those who, through faith and patience, inherit what has been promised." *Hebrews 6:12*

"[Do the right thing] even with an ulterior motive, for that habit of right doing will lead also to right motivation." *Talmud, Pesahim, 50b*

"These virtues are formed in man by his doing the actions." *Aristotle*

"For we grow in grace by applying grace and mercy—and in understanding as we try to understand. For it is the try, the attempt, that is the righteousness of man." *Edgar Cayce*

Your Spiritual Journey

"Search me, O God, and know my heart;
test me and know my thoughts.
See if there is any offensive way in me,
and guide me in the everlasting way." *Psalm 139:23-24*

"When we put God first, all other things fall into their proper place or drop out of our lives. Our love of the Lord will govern ... the demands on our time, the interests we pursue, and the order of our priorities." *Ezra Taft Benson*

"The moment one definitely commits oneself, then Providence moves too. All sorts of things occur to help one that would never have otherwise occurred ... unforeseen incidents and meetings and material assistance, which no man could have dreamed would have come his way." *Goethe*

"[E]verything happens for a reason, and there are no mistakes or coincidences." *Yehuda Berg*

"What is called chance is the instrument of Providence." *Horace Walpole*

"Be willing to accept the answers [to your prayers] no matter how or through whom they come. You may receive your answers from a stranger, an unlikely source, a random occurrence or even a billboard. The possibilities are endless." *Leo Carver*

"Whatever it is that stirs your soul, listen to that. Everything else is just noise." *Nicole Lyons*

"Sublime is the dignity of the soul, for to each a Guardian spirit is appointed from the beginning of its existence." *St. Jerome*

"Yet God has placed by the side of each a man's own Guardian Spirit, who is charged to watch over him .... So when you have shut the doors and made a darkness within, remember never to say that you are alone, for you are not alone; God is within, and your Guardian Spirit ...." *Epictetus*

"The Angels go in and out with us, having their eyes always fixed upon us and upon all that we are doing. If we stop anywhere, they stop also; if we go forth to walk, they bear us company; if we journey into another country, they follow us. Go where we will, by land or by sea, they are ever with us ...." *St. Augustine*

* * *

"Go in through the narrow gate. The gate to destruction is wide and the road that leads to it is easy, and there are many who travel it. But the gate to life is narrow and the way that leads to it is hard, and only a few ever find it." *Matthew 7:13-14*

"Two roads diverged in a wood, and I,
I took the one less traveled by,
And that has made all the difference." *Robert Frost*

Living on Earth

Life is what we make of it. "We either make ourselves happy or miserable. The amount of work is the same." *Carlos Castaneda*

Your lifetime is ticking away right now. "Time is your most precious gift because you only have a set amount of it. You can make more money, but you can't make more time. When you give someone your time, you are giving them a portion of your life that you'll never get back. Your time is your life." *Rick Warren*

"The key question to keep asking is, 'Are you spending your time on the right things?'" *Randy Pausch*

"Only put off until tomorrow what you are willing to die having left undone." *Pablo Picasso*

"Give me by all means the shorter and nobler life, instead of one that is longer but of less account!" *Epictetus*

"The measure of a life, after all, is not its duration, but its donation." *Corrie ten Boom*

"May you always be doing those good, kind things that show you are a child of God ...." *Philippians 1:11*

"[B]e blameless and pure, children of God without fault in a crooked and perverse generation, in which you shine as lights in the world." *Philippians 2:15*

"We try to live in such a way that no one will ever be offended or kept back from finding the Lord by the way we act, so that no one can find fault with us and blame it on the Lord. In fact, in everything we do we try to show that we are true ministers of God." *2 Corinthians 6:3-4*

"One candle can light a thousand other candles .... Be that candle." *James Altucher*

"Be the living expression of God's kindness: kindness in your face, kindness in your eyes, kindness in your smile." *St. Teresa of Calcutta*

"You are the light of the world—like a city on a hilltop that cannot be hidden." *Matthew 5:14*

"[S]et an example for the believers in speech, in conduct, in love, in faith and in purity." *1 Timothy 4:12*

"Be careful to conduct yourselves honorably among your neighbors who are nonbelievers." *1 Peter 2:12*

"I am my neighbor's bible[;] he is reading me." *Dorothy Keeling*

Living on Earth

"It is not living that matters, but living rightly." *Socrates*

"Ethics is knowing the difference between what you have a right to do and what is right to do." *Potter Stewart*

"Laws control the lesser man .... Right conduct controls the greater one." *Mark Twain*

"Wise men, though all laws were abolished, would lead the same lives." *Aristophanes*

"They demonstrate that God's law is written in their hearts ...." *Romans 2:15*

"Always do right. This will gratify some people and astonish the rest." *Mark Twain*

Never let the fear of embarrassment keep you from doing what you think God wants you to do. Don't worry about what other people think of your actions.

"So then the person who does not do the good he knows he should do is guilty of sin." *James 4:17*

"Do what you can, with what you have, where you are." *Theodore Roosevelt*

"Never decide to do nothing just because you can only do little. Do what you can." *Steve Maraboli*

"All that is necessary for the triumph of evil is for good men to do nothing." *Edmund Burke*

"Don't live like ignorant people, but like wise people, making the most of every opportunity, because these are evil days." *Ephesians 5:15-16*

"Our struggle is not against flesh and blood, but against the rulers, against the authorities, against the powers of darkness in this world, and against the spiritual forces of evil in the heavenly realms." *Ephesians 6:12*

"Have nothing to do with the worthless deeds of darkness, but rather expose them." *Ephesians 5:11*

"From now on, then, you must live the rest of your earthly lives controlled by God's will and not by human desires. For you have spent enough time in the past doing what godless people choose to do ...." *1 Peter 4:2-3*

"[T]hose who live according to the flesh have their outlook shaped by the things of the flesh, but those who live according to the Spirit have their outlook shaped by the things of the Spirit." *Romans 8:5*

"Right is right, even if everyone is against it; and wrong is wrong, even if everyone is for it." *William Penn*

"Do not follow the crowd in doing wrong." *Exodus 23:2*

"Associate with people who are likely to improve you." *Seneca*

"Hang out with people better than you and you will drift in that direction." *Warren Buffett*

"The pain of discipline is much less than the pain of regret." *Joel Osteen*

"If you struggle to resist temptation, surrounding yourself with people who possess a high degree of self-discipline can help…." *Amy Morin*

"Keep watching and praying so you don't fall into temptation, for the spirit is willing but the flesh is weak." *Matthew 26:41*

"You are tempted in the same way that everyone else is tempted. But God can be trusted not to let you be tempted too much, and he will provide a way out so that you may be able to endure it." *1 Corinthians 10:13*

"The most common way people give up their power is by thinking they don't have any." *Alice Walker*

"Anything you are addicted to controls you. To end the addiction, you must take back the power …." *Sandra Rogers*

"The important thing is not to retreat; you have to master yourself." *Olga Korbut*

"He who controls others may be powerful, but he who has mastered himself is mightier still." *Lao Tzu*

"I count him braver who overcomes his desires than he who conquers his enemies, for the hardest victory is the victory over self." *Aristotle*

"Don't wear yourself out trying to get rich." *Proverbs 23:4*

"Keep your lives free from the love of money and be content with what you have ...." *Hebrews 13:5*

"For four years, the Gates Foundation ... supported an effort by [Boston College's Center on Wealth and Philanthropy] to determine exactly how the American wealthy think and live .... The respondents turn out to be a generally dissatisfied lot, whose money has contributed to deep anxieties involving love, work, and family.... Most of them still do not consider themselves financially secure; for that, they say, they would require on average one-quarter more wealth than they currently possess." *Graeme Wood*

"Any man who does not think that what he has is more than ample is an unhappy man, even if he is the master of the whole world." *Epicurus*

"People who want to be rich fall into all sorts of temptations and traps. They are caught by foolish and harmful desires that drag them down to ruin and destruction. For the love of money is a source of all kinds of evil. Some people, craving money, have wandered from the true faith and pierced themselves with many sorrows." *1 Timothy 6:9-10*

"Do not be amazed when a man grows rich, when the splendor of his house increases. For when he dies, he will take nothing with him ...." *Psalm 49:16-17*

Living on Earth

"Watch out and guard yourself from all types of greed, because a man's life is not measured by the abundance of his possessions." *Luke 12:15*

"Do not store up for yourselves treasures on earth, where moth and rust destroy, and where thieves break in and steal. But store up for yourselves treasures in heaven, where moth and rust do not destroy, and where thieves do not break in and steal." *Matthew 6:19-20*

"For where your treasure is, there your heart will be also ...." *Matthew 6:21*

"No one can serve two masters. Either you will hate the one and love the other, or you will be devoted to the one and despise the other. You cannot serve both God and money." *Matthew 6:24*

"Am I now trying to win the approval of men or of God?" *Galatians 1:10*

"How you treated other people, not your wealth or accomplishments, is the most enduring impact you can leave on earth." *Rick Warren*

"Choose a good reputation over great riches; being held in high esteem is better than silver or gold." *Proverbs 22:1*

"What good will it be for a man to gain the whole world if he loses his soul? Is anything worth more than your soul?" *Matthew 16:26*

"Beware the barrenness of a busy life." *Socrates*

"Remember the Sabbath day by keeping it holy. Six days you shall labor and do all your work, but the seventh is a Sabbath to the Lord your God. On that day you shall not do any work ...." *Exodus 20:8-10*

"O gift of God, a perfect day, whereon no one shall work but play." *Henry Wadsworth Longfellow*

"This therefore seems good and fitting to me: that a man should eat and drink and enjoy the fruit of his labor he does under the sun during the few days of his life God has given him, because that is his reward." *Ecclesiastes 5:18*

"So one thing I want to say about life is don't be scared and don't hang back, and most of all, don't waste it." *Joan W. Blos*

Treat each day as if it were the last day of your life. "Teach us to number our days and recognize how few they are; help us to spend them as we should." *Psalm 90:12*

"I realized I had been experiencing the biggest tragedy of human existence: I was having the time of my life, and I didn't even know it." *Oren Miller*

"Enjoy the little things, for one day you may look back and realize they were the big things." *Robert Brault*

"Thank you, dear God, for this good life and forgive us if we do not love it enough." *Garrison Keillor*

Living on Earth

"If you want to know why you were placed on this planet, you must begin with God. You were born by his purpose and for his purpose." *Rick Warren*

"God places us in the world as his fellow workers ...." *Desmond Tutu*

"Do your best to win full approval in God's sight, as a worker who is not ashamed of his work ...." *2 Timothy 2:15*

"Whatever you do, work at it with all your heart, as working for the Lord, not for men." *Colossians 3:23*

"If you are wise and understand God's ways, prove it by living an honorable life, doing good works ...." *James 3:13*

"Our people must learn to devote themselves to doing what is good, in order to provide for urgent needs and not live unproductive lives." *Titus 3:14*

"We are but visitors on this planet. We are here for ninety or one hundred years at the very most. During that period, we must try to do something good, something useful with our lives." *The Dalai Lama*

"Therefore, as we have opportunity, let us work for the good of all ...." *Galatians 6:10*

"Always give yourselves fully to the work of the Lord, because you know that your labor in the Lord is not in vain." *1 Corinthians 15:58*

Every time a pebble is dropped in a pond, ripples spread out in every direction. In the same way, every act, good or bad, reverberates throughout the world. "What you do makes a difference, and you have to decide what kind of difference you want to make." *Jane Goodall*

"Whatever your hand finds to do, do it with all your might ...." *Ecclesiastes 9:10*

"Do what you can, with what you have, where you are." *Theodore Roosevelt*

"We must not, in trying to think about how we can make a big difference, ignore the small daily differences we can make which, over time, add up to big differences that we often cannot foresee." *Marian Wright Edelman*

"The drop hollows the stone not with force but by falling often." *Plutarch*

"Never be discouraged because good things get on so slowly here ...." *George MacDonald*

"You have to do the right thing. It may not be in your power, may not be in your time, that there'll be any fruit. But that doesn't mean you stop doing the right thing. You may never know what results come from your action. But if you do nothing, there will be no result." *Mahatma Gandhi*

"Never underestimate the power of a planted seed." *Origin Unknown*

Living on Earth

"The problem with our world is that we draw the circle of family too small." *St. Teresa of Calcutta*

"We live in a world in which we need to share responsibility. It's easy to say 'It's not my child, not my community, not my world, not my problem.' Then there are those who see the need and respond. I consider those people my heroes." *Fred Rogers*

"Let it never be said by future generations that indifference, cynicism or selfishness made us fail to live up to the ideals of humanism ...." *Nelson Mandela*

Do something meaningful with your life.

"You are not here merely to make a living. You are here in order to enable the world to live more amply, with greater vision, with a finer spirit of hope and achievement. You are here to enrich the world, and you impoverish yourself if you forget the errand." *Woodrow Wilson*

"Get up off of your knees. Come out of your churches, your mosques, your temples. God can hear your prayers for peace, justice, and hope in this broken world just fine while you're out creating peace, working for justice, and giving hope to this broken world.... Don't just pray for someone to do something. Be someone who does something. Don't just pray for answers. Be the answer." *L.R. Knost*

"[N]ever fail daily to do that good which lies next to your hand. Trust God to weave your little thread into the great web ...." *George MacDonald*

"You shall not pollute the land in which you live .... You shall not defile the land in which you live, in the midst of which I dwell ...." *Numbers 35:33-34*

"We have not inherited this earth from our parents to do with it what we will. We have borrowed it from our children and we must be careful to use it in their interests as well as our own." *Moses Henry Cass*

"The ultimate test of a moral society is the kind of world that it leaves to its children." *Dietrich Bonhoeffer*

"These goals—clean water for all, school for every child, medicine for the afflicted, an end to extreme and senseless poverty—these are not just any goals …. [T]hey are the Beatitudes for a globalised world." *Bono*

"Never doubt that a small group of thoughtful, committed citizens can change the world. Indeed, it is the only thing that ever has." *Margaret Meade*

"What inspires are the people who do something to better humanity in their own small corner of the world. They don't need headlines or accolades. They need only to know that they stepped up to make things better." *R. Kay Green*

"I expect to pass through this world but once. Any good therefore that I can do, or any kindness or abilities that I can show to any fellow creature, let me do it now. Let me not defer it or neglect it, for I shall not pass this way again." *William Penn*

Kindness and Compassion

"Kindness is the highest wisdom." *Juan de Palafox y Mendoza*

"Not one of you is a believer until he loves for his brother what he loves for himself." *40 Hadith of an Nawuwi 13*

"If you want others to be happy, practice compassion. If you want to be happy, practice compassion." *The Dalai Lama*

"[T]here should be no division in the body, but the members should have the same concern for one another. If one member suffers, all suffer ...." *1 Corinthians 12:25-26*

"Be devoted to one another in brotherly love." *Romans 12:10*

"The whole idea of compassion is based on a keen awareness of the interdependence of all these living beings, which are all part of one another, and all involved in one another." *Thomas Merton*

"If anyone ... sees a brother or sister in need but has no pity on them, how can the love of God be in that person?" *1 John 3:17*

"Self-absorption in all its forms kills empathy, let alone compassion." *Daniel Goleman*

"The self-centered inevitably become disrespectful; very often they do not even notice this, since 'respect' is precisely the ability to acknowledge others, to acknowledge their dignity, their condition, their needs." *Pope Francis*

"The self-centered person inevitably seeks his own interests; he thinks this is normal, even necessary." *Pope Francis*

"When we focus on ourselves, our world contracts as our problems and preoccupations loom large. But when we focus on others, our world expands. Our own problems drift to the periphery of the mind and so seem smaller ...." *Daniel Goleman*

"Be the living expression of God's kindness: kindness in your face, kindness in your eyes, kindness in your smile." *St. Teresa of Calcutta*

"If I can stop one heart from breaking, I shall not live in vain ...." *Emily Dickinson*

"In everything, treat others as you would want them to treat you. This is the essence of all that is taught in the law and [by] the prophets." *Matthew 7:12*

Kindness and Compassion

"Let us be concerned for one another—to help one another, to show love, and to do good." *Hebrews 10:24*

"Do not get tired of bringing the mercy of the Father to the poor, the sick, the abandoned ...." *Pope Francis*

"Remember those who are suffering, as though you were suffering as they are." *Hebrews 13:3*

Pray for folks who need help. "I pray for all of us, oppressor and friend, that together we may succeed in building a better world through human understanding and love, and that in doing so we may reduce the pain and suffering of all ...." *The Dalai Lama*

"She prayed for every friend and relative in need. Her home was peppered with post-its reminding her who to pray for and why." *Obituary of Betty Puckett Holland*

Pray for those who are carrying heavy burdens.
Pray for those with mental or physical disabilities.
Pray for those who are grieving.
Pray for those who have been hurt.
Pray for those who have been wronged.
Pray for those who are discouraged.
Pray for those who are depressed.
Pray for those who have lost hope.
Pray for those who don't know which way to turn.
Pray for those who have strayed from the right path.

"A guide, on finding a man who has lost his way, brings him back to the right path ...." *Epictetus*

"May you always be doing those good, kind things that show you are a child of God ...." *Philippians 1:11*

"Blessed are the merciful, for they will be shown mercy." *Matthew 5:7*

Treat customer-service agents like real human beings. Get organized before you begin talking with them. Don't take out your frustration on them. Be patient with them. Thank them.

Be considerate of the "little people" of the world—the ones who work the hardest but get paid the least. Be kind to them. Show them your gratitude.

"Truly I tell you, whatever you did for one of the least of these brothers and sisters of mine, you did for me." *Matthew 25:40*

"I was hungry and you gave me food, I was thirsty and you gave me something to drink, I was a stranger and you invited me in, I needed clothes and you clothed me, I was sick and you looked after me, I was in prison and you came to visit me." *Matthew 25:35-36*

"Too often we underestimate the power of a touch, a smile, a kind word, a listening ear, an honest compliment, or the smallest act of caring, all of which have the potential to turn a life around." *Leo Buscaglia*

"Be kinder than necessary, because everyone you meet is fighting some kind of battle." *Philo of Alexandria*

Kindness and Compassion

"No man is an island, entire of itself; every man is a piece of the continent, a part of the main.... Any man's death diminishes me, because I am involved in mankind; and therefore never send to know for whom the bell tolls; it tolls for thee." *John Donne*

"Washing one's hands of the conflict between the powerful and the powerless means to side with the powerful, not to be neutral." *Paula Freire*

"If you are neutral in situations of injustice, you have chosen the side of the oppressor." *Desmond Tutu*

"I swore never to be silent whenever wherever human beings endure suffering and humiliation. We must take sides. Neutrality helps the oppressor, never the victim. Silence encourages the tormentor, never the tormented. Sometimes we must interfere." *Elie Wiesel*

"If I witness someone being hurt physically, emotionally, mentally and/or spiritually, without hesitation I will intervene...and pray for the person/family/people involved." *Jo Randazzo*

"I don't speak because I have the power to speak; I speak because I don't have the power to remain silent." *Rav Kook*

"I have a voice, and I'm trying to use it to be the voice for all the innocent people who don't have one." *Enes Kanter*

"Speak up for those who have no voice, for the justice of all who are dispossessed." *Proverbs 31:8*

Generosity

"It's absolutely necessary to give back some of the lucky life you're living." *Massimo Bottura*

"You should each give, then, as you have decided, not with regret or out of a sense of duty, for God loves a cheerful giver." *2 Corinthians 9:7*

"They should be rich in good works and generous to those in need, always being ready to share with others." *1 Timothy 6:18*

"The believers were united in heart and mind, and they felt that what they owned was not their own, so they shared everything they had." *Acts 4:32*

"[A] poor widow came and put in two very small copper coins, worth only a few cents. Calling his disciples to him, Jesus said, 'Truly I tell you, this poor widow has given more than all the others. For they gave a tiny part of their surplus, but she, poor as she is, has given everything she had to live on.'" *Mark 12:42-44*

Generosity

"A bit of fragrance clings to the hand that gives flowers." *Chinese Proverb*

"One person gives freely, yet gains even more .... A generous man will prosper; he who refreshes others will himself be refreshed." *Proverbs 11:24-25*

"Give, and it will be given to you. A good measure, pressed down, shaken together and running over, will be poured into your lap. For with the measure you use, it will be measured to you." *Luke 6:38*

"Don't judge each day by the harvest you reap but by the seeds that you plant." *Robert Louis Stevenson (from "Admiral Guinea")*

"He who obtains has little. He who scatters has much." *Lao Tzu*

"What I gave, I have." *Persian Proverb*

"Do not withhold good from those to whom it is due, when it is in your power to do it." *Proverbs 3:27*

"Whoever is generous to the poor lends to the Lord, and he will repay him for his deed." *Proverbs 19:17*

"If anyone has material possessions and sees a brother or sister in need but has no pity on them, how can the love of God be in that person?" *1 John 3:17*

"Even as the Sun does not wait for prayers and incantations to rise, but shines forth and is welcomed by all, so also do not wait for clapping of hands and shouts and praise to do your duty. No, do good of your own accord, and you will be loved like the Sun." *Epictetus*

"Be careful not to perform your righteous acts before men to be seen by them. If you do, you will have no reward from your Father in heaven. So when you give to someone in need, do not announce it like the hypocrites do ... to call attention to their acts of charity!" *Matthew 6:1-2*

"When you give to those in need, don't let your left hand know what your right hand is doing ...." *Matthew 6:3*

Be generous with the gifts, time, praise, and attention you give to others.

"Rings and jewels are not gifts, but apologies for gifts. The only gift is a portion of thyself." *Ralph Waldo Emerson*

"If instead of a gem, or even a flower, we [were to] cast the gift of a loving thought into the heart of a friend, that would be giving as the angels give." *George MacDonald*

"Freely you have received; freely give." *Matthew 10:8*

"The purpose of life is to find your gift. The work of life is to develop it. The meaning of life is to give your gift away." *David Viscott*

Generosity

"Economists have been scrutinizing the links between income and happiness across nations, and psychologists have probed individuals to find out what really makes us tick when it comes to cash…. In short, this latest research suggests, wealth alone doesn't provide any guarantee of a good life. What matters a lot more than a big income is how people spend it. For instance, giving money away makes people a lot happier than lavishing it on themselves." *Andrew Blackman*

"It is more blessed to give than to receive." *Acts 20:35*

"While practicing generosity, we should always remember how very fortunate we are to have this opportunity." *Gomo Tulku*

Esteem and Humility

"I believe that the first test of a great man is his humility. I don't mean by humility, doubt of his power. But really great men have a curious feeling that the greatness is not of them, but through them. [T]hey see something divine in every other man and are endlessly, foolishly, incredibly merciful." *John Ruskin*

"Do nothing out of selfish ambition or vain conceit. Rather, in humility value others above yourselves." *Philippians 2:3*

"Instead, take the lowest place at the foot of the table. Then when your host sees you, he will come and say, 'Friend, we have a better place for you!' and you will be honored in front of all of the other guests." *Luke 14:10*

"For all those who exalt themselves will be humbled, but those who humble themselves will be raised up." *Luke 14:11*

"True humility is not thinking less of yourself; it is thinking of yourself less." *Rick Warren*

Esteem and Humility

"Pride goes before destruction, and a haughty spirit before a fall." *Proverbs 16:18*

"I fell from the Empire State Building. Nobody pushed me. I ... jumped. No parachute. I have no one to blame for myself. But what's changed is, I got my ass humbled. I paid a deep penalty. I've learned lessons. And I'm different." *Alex Rodriguez*

"Don't think too much of yourself." *Charles ("Mick") Michie*

"It is not the person who commends himself who is approved, but the person whom the Lord commends." *2 Corinthians 10:18*

"You shouldn't be made arrogant by something you didn't create yourself." *Bono*

"How can you be proud? You are just a branch; you don't support the roots—the roots support you." *Romans 11:18*

"[Love] does not boast, it is not proud." *1 Corinthians 13:4*

"I will be overlooked before I will boast." *Max Lucado*

"[I]t will come to pass that every braggart shall be found an ass." *William Shakespeare (from "All's Well That Ends Well")*

"The superior man is modest in his speech but exceeds in his actions." *Confucius*

"Do not be proud, but accept humble duties." *Romans 12:16*

"If you are wise and understand God's ways, prove it by living an honorable life, doing good works with the humility that comes from wisdom." *James 3:13*

"Choose a good reputation over great riches; being held in high esteem is better than silver or gold." *Proverbs 22:1*

"It is better to be humble in spirit with the lowly than to divide plunder with the proud." *Proverbs 16:19*

Never have a condescending attitude toward anyone. Treat people with humility and kindness in whatever circumstances you find yourself. It's shameful to act friendly toward a person in one situation but not another.

"There is nothing noble in being superior to your fellow man; true nobility is being superior to your former self." *Ernest Hemingway*

"I may not be where I need to be but I thank God I am not where I used to be." *Joyce Meyer*

"Be gentle with yourself. Be kind to yourself. You may not be perfect, but you are all you've got to work with." *Bhante Gunaratana*

Avoid measuring your self-worth by comparing yourself to others. God has given you gifts and endowed you with characteristics that are uniquely yours. He never intended for you to be exactly like anybody else.

Esteem and Humility

"Now I realize God doesn't want an orchestra of identical instruments all playing the same tune, so I let go of the status quo and decided to just be me. Besides, pretending to be a normal person day after day is exhausting!" *Suzy Toronto*

"Work at not needing approval from anyone and you will be free to be who you really are." *Rebbe Nachman of Breslov*

"I've just never cared what people think. It's more if I'm happy and I'm confident and feeling good, that's always been my thing." *Kelly Clarkson*

"I want to sing like the birds sing, not worrying about who hears or what they think." *Rumi*

Choosing Positivity

❖ ❖ ❖

"We all have finite time and energy. Any time we spend whining is unlikely to help us achieve our goals. And it won't make us happier." *Randy Pausch*

"Joy does not simply happen to us. We have to choose joy and keep choosing it every day." *Jesse Joseph*

"[W]e have the choice to become positive or negative. Simply by thinking positive thoughts and speaking positive words we attract positive energy." *Betty J. Eadie*

"The remarkable thing is we have a choice every day regarding the attitude we will embrace for that day. We cannot change our past…. We cannot change the inevitable. The only thing we can do is play on the one string we have, and that is our attitude." *Charles R. Swindoll*

"[E]verything can be taken from a man but one thing: The last of the human freedoms—to choose one's attitude in any given set of circumstances; to choose one's own way." *Viktor Frankl*

Choosing Positivity

"A pessimist is a man who takes every opportunity of seeing a difficulty, but the optimist is he who sees in every difficulty an opportunity." *F.W. Cole*

"The person who says it cannot be done should not interrupt the person who is doing it." *Origin Unknown*

"Optimism is essential to achievement." *Nicholas Murray Butler*

"Optimism doesn't wait on facts. It deals with prospects. Pessimism is a waste of time." *Norman Cousins*

"Optimism is a muscle that gets stronger with use." *Robin Roberts*

"Remember to look at your glass half full and not half empty." *Mattie Stepanek*

"Look at the sunny side of everything. Think only of the best, work only for the best, and expect only the best." *Christian D. Larsen*

"A positive mind anticipates … a successful outcome of every situation and action." *Anurag Aggarwal*

"Be bold in your caring, be bold in your dreaming and above all else, always do your best." *George H.W. Bush*

Swing for the fences! "I swing big, with everything I've got. I hit big or I miss big. I like to live as big as I can." *Babe Ruth*

"You cannot have a positive life and a negative mind." *Joyce Meyer*

"If you expect the battle to be insurmountable, you've met the enemy. It's you." *Khang Kijarro Nguyen*

"Your thoughts greatly influence how you feel and behave. In fact, your inner monologue has a tendency to become a self-fulfilling prophecy." *Amy Morin*

"Both hope and despair are self-fulfilling prophecies." *Shlomo Breznitz*

"We either make ourselves happy or miserable. The amount of work is the same." *Carlos Castaneda*

"Change your thoughts and you change your world." *Norman Vincent Peale*

"Most people are about as happy as they make up their minds to be." *Abraham Lincoln*

"A happy person is not a person in a certain set of circumstances, but rather a person with a certain set of attitudes." *Hugh Downs*

"We are shaped by our thoughts; we become what we think. When the mind is pure, joy follows like a shadow that never leaves." *The Buddha*

"For as a man thinks in his heart, so is he." *Proverbs 23:7*

Choosing Positivity

Replace net negatives in your life with net positives.

"Life may bring you to your knees; pray. Then GET UP and participate in the answer." *Steve Maraboli*

"Above all, be the heroine of your life, not the victim." *Nora Ephron*

"Write the bad things that are done to you in sand, but write the good things that happen to you on a piece of marble." *Arabic Proverb*

"Turn your face to the sun and the shadows fall behind you." *Maori Proverb*

"I am fundamentally an optimist.... Part of being optimistic is keeping one's head pointed toward the sun, one's feet moving forward. There were many dark moments when my faith in humanity was sorely tested, but I would not and could not give myself up to despair." *Nelson Mandela*

"If I am happy in spite of my deprivations, if my happiness is so deep that it is a faith, so thoughtful that it becomes a philosophy of life. If, in short, I am an optimist, my testimony to the creed of optimism is worth hearing." *Helen Keller*

"Although the world is full of suffering, it is full also of the overcoming of it. My optimism, then, does not rest on the absence of evil, but on a glad belief in the preponderance of good and a willing effort always to cooperate with the good, that it may prevail." *Helen Keller*

"In spite of everything I still believe that people are really good at heart. I simply can't build up my hopes on a foundation consisting of confusion, misery, and death. I see the world gradually being turned into a wilderness, I hear the ever approaching thunder, which will destroy us too, I can feel the sufferings of millions and yet, if I look up into the heavens, I think that it will all come right, that this cruelty too will end, and that peace and tranquility will return again." *Anne Frank*

Acceptance and Tolerance

❖ ❖ ❖

"While I know myself as a creation of God, I am also obligated to realize and remember that everyone else and everything else are also God's creation." *Maya Angelou*

"We hold these truths to be self-evident, that all men are created equal, that they are endowed by their Creator with certain unalienable Rights ...." *United States Declaration of Independence*

From God's perspective, how a person is regarded on Earth is immaterial. "In this new life one's nationality or race or education or social position is unimportant; such things mean nothing." *Colossians 3:11*

"God does not judge as people judge. They look at the outward appearance, but the Lord looks at the heart." *1 Samuel 16:7*

"I now realize how true it is that God does not show favoritism but welcomes from every nation the one who fears him and does what is right." *Acts 10:34-35*

"We are all formed of frailty and error; let us pardon reciprocally each other's folly ...." *Voltaire*

"Tolerance is possessing a heart or a spirit that gives room at all times for people's weakness and imperfection[,] fostering peace and promoting friendship." *John Ibenu*

"Let any one of you who is without sin throw the first stone ...." *John 8:7*

"Whose house is of glass, must not throw stones at another." *George Herbert*

"Do not judge others or you too will be judged. For with the ... measure you use, it will be measured to you. Why, then, do you look at the speck in your brother's eye and pay no attention to the log in your own eye?" *Matthew 7:1-3*

"Or why do you treat them with contempt? For we will all stand before God's judgment seat." *Romans 14:10*

"There is only one Lawgiver and Judge, the One who is able to save and destroy. Who are you to judge your neighbor?" *James 4:12*

"He will not judge by appearance or what he hears; he will judge the poor fairly and defend the rights of the helpless." *Isaiah 11:3-4*

"If someone ... searches for the Lord and has goodwill, who am I to judge?" *Pope Francis*

Acceptance and Tolerance

"No one is born hating another person because of the color of his skin, or his background, or his religion. People must learn to hate, and if they can learn to hate, they can be taught to love, for love comes more naturally to the human heart than its opposite." *Nelson Mandela*

"The first day I stepped on the set of 'Selma,' I began to feel like this was bigger than a movie. As I got to know the people of the Civil Rights movement, I realized I am the hopeful black woman who was denied her right to vote. I am the caring white supporter killed on the front lines of freedom.... 'Selma' has awakened my humanity …. We look to the future, and we want to create a better world. Now is our time to change the world." *Common*

"The responsibility of tolerance lies with those who have the wider vision." *George Eliot*

"The test of courage comes when we are in the minority. The test of tolerance comes when we are in the majority." *Ralph W. Sockman*

"If man is to survive, he will have learned to take a delight in the essential differences between men and between cultures. He will learn that differences in ideas and attitudes are a delight, part of life's exciting variety, not something to fear." *Gene Roddenberry*

"Now I realize God doesn't want an orchestra of identical instruments all playing the same tune ...." *Suzy Toronto*

"Tolerance implies no lack of commitment to one's own beliefs. Rather it condemns the oppression or persecution of others." *John F. Kennedy*

"An attack on any faith is an attack on all of our faiths." *Barack Obama*

"Any religion, or denomination, that attempts to restrict your association with others not of your particular belief is worshiping their idea of God, not God." *Sandra Rogers*

"I appeal to you, brothers, to watch out for those who cause divisions and create obstacles contrary to the doctrine that you have been taught." *Romans 16:17*

"A person who thinks only about building walls, wherever they may be, and not building bridges, is not Christian." *Pope Francis*

"There are already enough critical, judgmental people in the world. Let's be people who lift up others and restore them." *Joel Osteen*

"People, I just want to say, you know, can we all get along?" *Rodney King*

Encouragement

❖ ❖ ❖

"Let your hook be always cast; in the pool where you least expect it, there will be a fish." *Ovid*

"Even though the future seems far away, it is actually beginning right now." *Mattie Stepanek*

"So if you're feeling lost or stuck, remember that it is temporary. The person you are today won't be the person you are tomorrow, in a week, or in a month." *Anjana Bala*

"In the midst of chaos, I found there was, within me, an invincible calm.... In the midst of winter, I found there was, within me, an invincible summer. And that makes me happy. For it says that no matter how hard the world pushes against me, within me, there's something stronger—something better, pushing right back." *Albert Camus*

"While there is life, there is hope." *Erasmus*

"Keep a green tree alive in your heart and a songbird may come to sing there." *Chinese Proverb*

"One of the things I learned the hard way was that it doesn't pay to get discouraged. Keeping busy and making optimism a way of life can restore your faith in yourself." *Lucille Ball*

"Those who hope in the Lord will renew their strength. They will soar on wings like eagles; they will run and not grow weary, they will walk and not be faint." *Isaiah 40:31*

"'For I know the plans I have for you,' declares the Lord, ... 'plans to give you hope and a future.'" *Jeremiah 29:11*

"We are products of our past, but we don't have to be prisoners of it." *Rick Warren*

"Cryin' about a bad past is a waste of good tears." *Gladiola Montana*

"Yesterday is not ours to recover, but tomorrow is ours to win or to lose." *Lyndon B. Johnson*

"I focus on this one thing: forgetting what is past and looking forward to what lies ahead." *Philippians 3:13*

"Do not call to mind the former things,
or dwell on things of the past.
See, I am doing a new thing!
Now it springs up;
do you not perceive it?
I am making a way in the desert
and streams in the wasteland." *Isaiah 43:18-19*

Encouragement

"You can do so much more than you think you can." *Jessie Graff*

"Our greatest glory is not in never falling, but in rising every time we fall." *Confucius*

"Never give up. That's a given. You always fight." *Tiger Woods*

"If you have made mistakes, even serious ones, there is always another chance for you. What we call failure is not the falling down, but the staying down." *Mary Pickford*

"Never confuse a single defeat with a final defeat." *F. Scott Fitzgerald*

"Fall seven times, stand up eight." *Japanese Proverb*

"Many of us give up when we fail. We allow an attitude of defeat to take over.... But, have you ever wondered what would have happened if you had just tried one more time, or two more times?" *Catherine Pulsifer*

"When you [think you] have exhausted all possibilities, remember this: you haven't." *Thomas Edison*

"When you get into a tight place
and everything goes against you,
till it seems as though you could not hang on
a minute longer,
never give up then,
for that is just the place and time
that the tide will turn." *Harriet Beecher Stowe*

"It is not because things are difficult that we do not dare; it is because we do not dare that they are difficult." *Seneca*

"In the midst of difficulty lies opportunity." *Albert Einstein*

"A pessimist is a man who takes every opportunity of seeing a difficulty, but the optimist is he who sees in every difficulty an opportunity." *F.W. Cole*

"Don't live like ignorant people, but like wise people, making the most of every opportunity ...." *Ephesians 5:15-16*

"A great deal of talent is lost to the world for want of a little courage." *Sydney Smith*

"You miss 100% of the shots you don't take." *Wayne Gretzky*

"Never give up on a dream just because of the length of time it will take to accomplish it." *H. Jackson Brown Jr.*

"A journey of a thousand miles begins with a single step." *Lao Tzu*

"We have, in short, somehow become convinced that we need to tackle the whole problem, all at once. But the truth is that we don't." *Malcolm Gladwell*

"The man who removes a mountain begins by carrying away small stones." *William Faulkner*

Encouragement

"You've got to go out on a limb sometimes because that's where the fruit is." *Will Rogers*

"You see things; and you say 'Why?' But I dream things that never were; and I say 'Why not?'" *George Bernard Shaw*

Set some lofty goals for yourself. "If a man knows not to which port he sails, no wind is favorable." *Seneca*

"[P]lant your own gardens and decorate your own soul, instead of waiting for someone to bring you flowers." *Jorge Luis Borges*

"If our gift is to ... encourage others, we should do so ...." *Romans 12:6-8*

"Therefore encourage one another and build each other up, just as in fact you are doing." *1 Thessalonians 5:11*

"Never stop fighting, and do all you can to lift up everyone around you." *Prince Harry, Duke of Sussex*

"Now may ... God our Father, who by grace has loved us and given us eternal comfort and good hope, encourage your hearts and strengthen you in every good word and deed." *2 Thessalonians 2:16-17*

Helpfulness

❖ ❖ ❖

"Let each of you look not only to his own interests, but also to the interests of others." *Philippians 2:4*

"Not for ourselves alone are we born." *Cicero*

"We who are strong have an obligation to help the weak carry their burdens, and not to please ourselves." *Romans 15:1*

"Therefore, as we have opportunity, let us work for the good of all ...." *Galatians 6:10*

"Help one at a time, and always start with those nearest you." *St. Teresa of Calcutta*

"Each of you should use whatever gift you have received to serve others, as a faithful administrator of God's grace in its various forms." *1 Peter 4:10*

"The greatest among you must be a servant." *Matthew 23:11*

Helpfulness

"Help carry one another's burdens ...." *Galatians 6:2*

Never let laziness, being "in a hurry," or the fear of appearing "uncool" keep you from stopping and offering your assistance when it seems to be needed. As long as you aren't doing anything wrong, don't worry about what other people think about your actions.

Rescue innocent people from awkward situations when you see opportunities to do that.

Take the time to be helpful to newcomers, outsiders, and immigrants. Consider what it must be like to be a "stranger in a strange land."

"Do not forget to show hospitality to strangers, for by doing so some people have helped angels without knowing it." *Hebrews 13:2*

"Never reach out your hand unless you're willing to extend an arm." *Pope Paul VI*

"There is no exercise better for the heart than reaching down and lifting people up." *John Holmes*

"Therefore encourage one another and build each other up, just as in fact you are doing." *1 Thessalonians 5:11*

"As human beings, our job in life is to help people realize how rare and valuable each one of us really is, that each of us has something that no one else has—or ever will have—something inside that is unique to all time." *Fred Rogers*

Help out the "little people" of this world. Do what you can to make life a little easier for those who serve others. Have mercy on them! For example:

Don't go into a business so close to closing time that you cause someone to have to stay late to help you.

When you've finished shopping, return your shopping cart to an appropriate area (or, even better, return an abandoned cart that you didn't even use).

If you take or knock items off a shelf or rack in a store or at a market, put them back where they belong if you don't intend to buy them.

To the extent possible, don't cause someone to have to straighten up or clean up after you. And don't allow your group to leave behind a big mess for the cleaning folks. At least mitigate the damage before moving on.

Pick up litter when leaving a park or other community space; leave it a little (or a lot) nicer than you found it.

Give trash-collection and recycling workers a break. Don't put out your trash or recycling bins on trash-collection day if there's hardly anything in them. Don't put anything into your recycling bins that some poor soul is going to have to fish out later on.

If you are mailing big packages or lots of packages, drop them off at the post office instead of loading up your mail carrier.

Helpfulness

When you see something hazardous lying on or obstructing the road, remove it or at least move it out of the way if you can do that safely. Otherwise, take a minute to notify the responsible authorities about it.

Report problems with potholes, street signs, etc.

If you witness an accident, take the time to pull over to a safe area and offer to help in any way you can. Before leaving the site, provide your contact information in case your statement or testimony is needed later on.

Give other drivers a break when you can. Drive as though those around you are friends and loved ones.

When other drivers give *you* a break in traffic, give them a wave of appreciation!

In every situation, show your appreciation to those who have a helpful spirit.

Peace

❖ ❖ ❖

"A heart at peace revives the body …." *Proverbs 14:30*

"If it is possible, as far as it depends on you, live at peace with everyone." *Romans 12:18*

"Make every effort to keep the unity of the Spirit through the bond of peace." *Ephesians 4:3*

"May God, who gives patience and encouragement, help you live in complete harmony with each other …." *Romans 15:5*

"Let us therefore make every effort to do what leads to peace and to building each other up." *Romans 14:19*

"Blessed are the peacemakers, for they will be called the children of God." *Matthew 5:9*

"And goodness is the harvest that is produced from the seeds the peacemakers plant in peace." *James 3:18*

Peace

"Be beautiful inside, in your hearts, with the unfading beauty of a gentle and quiet spirit which is so precious to God." *1 Peter 3:4*

"[L]ive a quiet and peaceful life with all reverence toward God and with proper conduct." *1 Timothy 2:2*

"Keep yourself connected to the peace that lives at the heart of who you are." *Origin Unknown*

"You will keep in perfect peace all who trust in you, all whose thoughts are focused on you." *Isaiah 26:3*

"Don't be anxious about anything, but in every situation, by prayer and ... with thanksgiving, present your requests to God. Then you will experience God's peace, which exceeds anything we can understand." *Philippians 4:6-7*

"May the Lord show you his favor and give you his peace." *Numbers 6:26*

Guarding Your Thoughts and Words

❖ ❖ ❖

"As a man thinks in his heart, so is he." *Proverbs 23:7*

"Such as are your habitual thoughts, such also will be the character of your mind; for the soul is dyed by the thoughts." *Marcus Aurelius*

"A good man brings good things out of the good stored up in his heart, and an evil man brings evil things out of the evil stored up in his heart. For the mouth speaks what the heart is full of." *Luke 6:45*

"If we understood the power of our thoughts, we would guard them more closely. If we understood the awesome power of our words, we would prefer silence to almost anything negative." *Betty J. Eadie*

"Your worst enemy cannot harm you as much as your own unguarded thoughts." *The Buddha*

"[W]hatever is true, whatever is honorable, whatever is just, whatever is pure, whatever is lovely, whatever is commendable, if there is any excellence, if there is anything worthy of praise, think on these things." *Philippians 4:8*

Guarding Your Thoughts and Words

"Set a guard over my mouth, O Lord; keep watch over the door of my lips." *Psalm 141:3*

"Those who consider themselves religious and yet do not keep a tight rein on their tongues deceive themselves, and their religion is worthless." *James 1:26*

"[T]he human tongue is a beast that few can master. It strains constantly to break out of its cage, and if it is not tamed, it will run wild and cause you grief." *Robert Greene*

"Those who guard their lips preserve their lives, but those who speak rashly will come to ruin." *Proverbs 13:3*

"There is no virtuous necessity for expressing all the dislikes that flash across your feelings. Very often it is necessary as a matter of virtue to spare others the hurt that would be given by freely expressing your opinion." *Lawrence G. Lovasik*

"Before you speak ask yourself if what you are going to say is true, is kind, is necessary, is helpful." *Bernard Meltzer*

"Complaining not only ruins everybody else's day, it ruins the complainer's day, too." *Dennis Prager*

"Remember not only to say the right thing in the right place, but far more difficult still, to leave unsaid the wrong thing at the tempting moment." *Benjamin Franklin*

"The tongue is a small thing, but what enormous damage it can do." *James 3:5*

"An ungodly man digs up evil, and his speech is like a scorching fire." *Proverbs 16:27*

"The words of the reckless pierce like swords, but the tongue of the wise brings healing." *Proverbs 12:18*

"The healing tongue is a tree of life, but a perverse tongue breaks the spirit." *Proverbs 15:4*

"A perverse person stirs up conflict, and a gossip separates close friends." *Proverbs 16:28*

"Without wood, a fire goes out; without a gossip, conflict dies down." *Proverbs 26:20*

"A gentle answer turns away wrath, but a harsh one stirs it up." *Proverbs 15:1*

"Raise your words, not your voice. It is rain that grows flowers, not thunder." *Rumi*

"Tell them not to speak evil of anyone, but to be peaceful and friendly, and always to show a gentle attitude toward everyone." *Titus 3:2*

"There is so much good in the worst of us, and so much bad in the best of us, it doesn't behoove any of us to speak evil of the rest of us." *Edgar Cayce*

Guarding Your Thoughts and Words

"Keep your tongue from evil and your lips from deceitful speech." *Psalm 34:13*

"Each of you must put off falsehood and speak truthfully ...." *Ephesians 4:25*

Don't make ignorant assertions that undermine your credibility. "It is unwise to be too sure of one's own wisdom." *Mahatma Gandhi*

"Men cease to think when they think they know it all." *Horace*

"Those who think they know it all have no way of finding out that they don't." *Leo Buscaglia*

"The peculiar evil of silencing the expression of an opinion is that it [robs] those who dissent from the opinion, still more than those who hold it. If the opinion is right, they are deprived of the opportunity of exchanging error for truth ...." *John Stuart Mill*

"We have two ears and only one tongue in order that we may hear more and speak less." *Diogenes*

"Everyone should be quick to listen, slow to speak and slow to become angry." *James 1:19*

"Better to remain silent and be thought a fool than to speak out and remove all doubt." *Abraham Lincoln*

Don't let anybody pressure you or lure you into discussions that you don't want any part of.

"My rookie year I kind of talked junk to everybody. In the middle of the game I started talking to Tim [Duncan] .... I just kept talking junk to him and he kept staring at me. At that point I realized during the rest of my career that I might as well not talk to him. Either, one, he is not going to talk back because he has no respect for me. Or, two, he is not going to talk back because that is who he is. Or, three, both. I figured then that was the last time I would talk junk to Tim. And that was the last time." *Draymond Green*

"Don't waste your breath on fools ...." *Proverbs 23:9*

"Ignoring an insult is a foolproof way to keep from getting bogged down in someone else's negative energy, or even in your own." *Elaine St. James*

"Do not repay evil with evil or insult with insult, but with blessing ...." *1 Peter 3:9*

"Do not use harmful words, but only helpful words, the kind that build up and provide what is needed, so that what you say will benefit those who hear you. And do not make God's Holy Spirit sad …." *Ephesians 4:29-30*

"Nor should there be obscenity, foolish talk or coarse joking, which are out of place, but rather thanksgiving." *Ephesians 5:4*

Guarding Your Thoughts and Words

"You shall not misuse the name of the Lord your God, for the Lord will not hold anyone guiltless who misuses his name." *Exodus 20:7*

"You can be sure that on the Judgment Day everyone will have to give account of every careless word he has ever spoken." *Matthew 12:36*

"The words you say will either acquit you or condemn you." *Matthew 12:37*

"May the words of my mouth and the meditation of my heart be pleasing in your sight, O Lord, my rock and my redeemer." *Psalm 19:14*

Revenge

❖ ❖ ❖

"Certainly, in taking revenge, a man is but even with his enemy; but in passing it over, he is superior ...." *Francis Bacon*

"You will achieve more in this world through acts of mercy than you will through acts of retribution." *Nelson Mandela*

"You have heard that it was said, 'Love your neighbor and hate your enemy.' But I tell you, love your enemies and pray for those who persecute you." *Matthew 5:43-44*

"Darkness cannot drive out darkness; only light can do that. Hate cannot drive out hate; only love can do that." *Martin Luther King Jr.*

"If your enemy is hungry, feed him; if the is thirsty, give him something to drink .... Do not be overcome by evil, but overcome evil with good." *Romans 12:20-21*

"It is better for my enemy to see good in me than for me to see evil in him." *Yiddish Proverb*

Revenge

"The Lord loves justice and will not forsake his faithful ones." *Psalm 37:28*

"Beloved, never avenge yourselves, but leave it to the wrath of God. 'Vengeance is mine; I will repay,' says the Lord." *Romans 12:19*

If you've been treated badly, don't respond with bad behavior of your own. Don't forfeit your soul in pursuit of retribution.

"We should not seek revenge on those who have committed crimes against us, or reply to their crimes with other crimes. We should reflect that by the law of karma, they are in danger of lowly and miserable lives to come, and that our duty to them, as to every being, is to help them ...." *The Dalai Lama*

Forgiveness

❖ ❖ ❖

"Love keeps no record of wrongs." *1 Corinthians 13:5*

"Get rid of all bitterness, rage and anger, brawling and slander, along with every form of malice. Be kind and compassionate to one another, forgiving each other ...." *Ephesians 4:31-32*

"If any man was wronged by another and he neither rebukes, nor hates, nor bears a grudge against him, but forgives him with his whole heart, this is a saintly virtue." *Code of Jewish Law*

"The highest exercise of charity is charity towards the uncharitable." *J.S. Buckminster*

Holding a grudge just adds more weight to the load you're already carrying. "Even here, love, and love alone, frees us. Above all it frees us from the mortal danger of pent-up anger, of that smoldering anger which makes us brood over wrongs we have received." *Pope Francis*

"To forgive is to set a prisoner free and discover that the prisoner was you." *Lewis B. Smedes*

Forgiveness

"Be gentle and ready to forgive; never hold grudges." *Colossians 3:13*

"So instead, you ought to forgive and comfort him, so that he will not be overwhelmed by excessive sorrow." *2 Corinthians 2:7*

"To forgive, avoid ruminating on thoughts of being wronged. Rather, trust the power of forgiveness to heal the hurt and pain." *Tony Fahkry*

Instead of opting for bitterness, choose forgiveness. "I choose to shake off the old; I choose to forgive." *Joel Osteen*

"You either get bitter or you get better. It's that simple." *Josh Shipp*

"I had to learn to forgive…. I had to let go, to let God deal with it. No one wants to be mad in their own house. I didn't want to be angry my whole life. It takes so much energy out of you to be mean." *Rodney King*

"When we take the ugliness out of our heart and learn to forgive, God will get us where we need to be." *Marietta Jaeger Lane*

"The more a man knows, the more he forgives." *Confucius*

"Be merciful, just as your Father is merciful. [D]o not condemn others, and God will not condemn you; forgive others, and God will forgive you." *Luke 6:36-37*

"If my people ... will humble themselves and pray and seek my face and turn from their wicked ways, then I will hear from heaven, and I will forgive their sin and will heal their land." *2 Chronicles 7:14*

God embraces everybody who comes back into the fold.

"There is nothing you've done wrong that is too big for God to fix." *Joyce Meyer*

"Draw near to God and he will draw near to you." *James 4:8*

"I acknowledged my sin to You. I didn't whitewash my wrongdoing. I said, 'I will confess my transgressions to The Lord,' and You took away the iniquity of my sin." *Psalm 32:5*

"He is merciful and tender toward those who don't deserve it; he is slow to get angry and full of kindness and love. He never bears a grudge or remains angry forever." *Psalm 103:8-9*

Faith

❖ ❖ ❖

"Begin to weave and God will give the thread." *German Proverb*

"The moment one definitely commits oneself, then Providence moves, too. All sorts of things occur to help one that would never have otherwise occurred ... unforeseen incidents and meetings and material assistance, which no man could have dreamed would have come his way." *Goethe*

"The moment we believe, the gates are opened, and a flood of energy is unleashed." *Shlomo Breznitz*

"Big faith equals big results. Big dreams, plus big thinking, plus big faith, plus big effort—that is the formula by which things are done ... and by which big difficulties are overcome." *Norman Vincent Peale*

"[Y]ou have to trust that the dots will somehow connect in your future. You have to trust in something—your gut, destiny, life, karma, whatever. This approach has never let me down, and it has made all the difference in my life." *Steve Jobs*

"So do not throw away this confident trust in the Lord. Remember the great reward it brings you!" *Hebrews 10:35*

"Now faith is confidence in what we hope for and assurance about what we cannot see." *Hebrews 11:1*

"For we walk by faith, not by sight." *2 Corinthians 5:7*

"He did not waver in unbelief about God's promise but was strengthened in his faith and gave glory to God." *Romans 4:20*

"I have not lost faith in God. I have moments of anger and protest. Sometimes I've been closer to him for that reason." *Elie Wiesel*

"You have to have faith that there is a reason you go through certain things." *Carol Burnett*

"My righteous one shall live by faith, and if he shrinks back my soul has no pleasure in him." *Hebrews 10:38*

"[Y]ou must believe and not doubt, because the one who doubts is like a wave of the sea, blown and tossed by the wind." *James 1:6*

"Now without faith it is impossible to please God, for whoever comes to him must believe that he exists and that he rewards those who seek him." *Hebrews 11:6*

Faith

"Faith consists in believing when it is beyond the power of reason to believe. It is not enough that a thing be possible for it to be believed." *Voltaire*

"The time will come when diligent research over long periods will bring to light things which now lie hidden.... There will come a time when our descendants will be amazed that we did not know things that are so plain to them." *Seneca*

"Miracles do not happen in contradiction to nature, but only in contradiction to that which is known to us of nature." *St. Augustine*

"I do not believe in the God of the theologians; but that there is a Supreme Intelligence I do not doubt." *Thomas Edison*

"[O]ur actual knowledge of the laws [of nature] is only imperfect and fragmentary, so that, actually, the belief in the existence of basic all-embracing laws in nature also rests on a sort of faith.... But on the other hand, everyone who is seriously involved in the pursuit of science becomes convinced that a Spirit is manifest in the laws of the universe—a Spirit vastly superior to that of man, and one in the face of which we with our modest powers must feel humble." *Albert Einstein*

"Any one thing in the creation is sufficient to demonstrate a Providence to a humble and grateful mind." *Epictetus*

Parents and Parenting

❖ ❖ ❖

Beginning when they're very young, teach your children about God. "Be very careful never to forget what you have seen God doing for you. May his miracles have a deep and permanent effect upon your lives! Tell your children and your grandchildren about the glorious miracles he did." *Deuteronomy 4:9*

Set a good example for your children. "Live so that when your children think of fairness, caring, and integrity, they think of you." *H. Jackson Brown Jr.*

"[I]f you cause one of these little ones who trusts in me to fall into sin, it would be better for you to be thrown into the sea with a large millstone hung around your neck." *Mark 9:42*

"Things that cause people to stumble are bound to come, but woe to anyone through whom they come." *Luke 17:1*

"Be careful ... that the exercise of your rights does not become a stumbling block to the weak." *1 Corinthians 8:9*

Parents and Parenting

"You can only prepare the child for the path, not the path for the child." *Jen Hatmaker*

"It makes no small difference, therefore, whether a man be trained in his youth up in this way or that, but a great difference, or rather all the difference." *Aristotle*

"Just as the twig is bent, the tree's inclined." *Alexander Pope*

"Train a child in the way he should go, and when he is old he will not turn from it." *Proverbs 22:6*

"[B]ring them up in the training and instruction of the Lord." *Ephesians 6:4*

Never reward a child's negative behavior by giving in to it. "Those who love their children care enough to discipline them." *Proverbs 13:24*

"Discipline your son and you can always be proud of him." *Proverbs 29:17*

"There's a lot of talk these days about giving children self-esteem. It's not something you can give; it's something they have to build.... You give them something they can't do, they work hard until they find they can do it, and you just keep repeating the process." *Randy Pausch*

"Teach your children the pride, satisfaction, and dignity of doing any job well." *H. Jackson Brown Jr.*

"They should be rich in good works and generous to those in need, always being ready to share with others." *1 Timothy 6:18*

"[C]hildren must early learn the beauty of generosity." *Ohiyesa*

"Tell them not to speak evil of anyone, but to be peaceful and friendly, and always to show a gentle attitude toward everyone." *Titus 3:2*

"Fathers, do not exasperate your children or provoke them to anger by the way you treat them." *Ephesians 6:4*

Try not to put impossibly heavy burdens on your children.

Whenever you realize you've said or done something wrong to your children, acknowledge your mistake and apologize to them.

Even if you haven't been such a great parent in the past, that doesn't mean you can't *ever* be a good one. "There is nothing you've done wrong that is too big for God to fix. He can truly make all things work together for good, not only for you but for your children too." *Joyce Meyer*

"[P]arenting is hard. Forget about crafting the perfect family image. We'll all mess up more times than we can count.... The Lord knows, we get so many things wrong as parents. Then there are those beautiful, blessed moments we get things right." *Jen Hatmaker*

Parents and Parenting

"The child is the beauty of God present in the world, that greatest gift to a family." *St. Teresa of Calcutta*

Set aside some of your precious time for your precious children. You'll never get a do-over for these days.

Look at the things your children want to show to you. Be the audience when they want to perform for you.

Play with your kids. "O gift of God, a perfect day, whereon no one shall work but play." *Henry Wadsworth Longfellow*

Whenever you're spending "quality" time with your children, make sure that you're actually paying attention to them. Do your best to focus only on them during those times that you've set aside for them.

Demonstrate to your children that you care about what they have to say by being a good listener.

"Because I came to realize that a child can hold an important thought, something they want to say to their mom and dad, maybe for 12 or 24 hours, and then it's gone. And when it's gone, it's gone. And it all adds up." *Joe Biden*

"Somebody said to me that the best thing to do [during kids' teenage years] is not say very much. Give them guidance as they're growing up before they're teenagers, and then when it's their turn to try things and express things, you just have to listen a lot—just really, really listen." *Angelina Jolie*

"[T]he test of a civilization is in the way that it cares for its helpless members." *Pearl S. Buck*

Be devoted to your parents, especially if they're elderly or in poor health.

Enrich your life by spending time with and learning from your parents.

Don't talk disrespectfully to—or about—your parents.

Forgive your parents for their faults and deficiencies.

Forgive your parents for mistakes they made with you. "Honor your father and mother …." *Exodus 20:12*

Live in a way that makes your parents and grandparents proud of you. Don't disappoint them or bring shame on them by behaving badly. Try to perpetuate in yourself, and teach to your children and your grandchildren, the values that they passed on to you.

Remember that the hopes and dreams of generations rest upon your shoulders.

On the Job

❖ ❖ ❖

"Whatever you do, work at it with all your heart, as working for the Lord, not for men." *Colossians 3:23*

"You are not here merely to make a living. You are here in order to enable the world to live more amply, with greater vision, with a finer spirit of hope and achievement. You are here to enrich the world, and you impoverish yourself if you forget the errand." *Woodrow Wilson*

"If your actions inspire others to dream more, learn more, do more and become more, you are a leader." *John Quincy Adams*

"Don't chase money. If you are the best in your field, money will find you." *Thomas J. Stanley*

"If we are delighting customers, eliminating unnecessary costs, and improving our products and services, we gain strength. But if we treat customers with indifference or tolerate bloat, our businesses will wither. On daily basis, the effects of our actions are imperceptible; cumulatively, though, their consequences are enormous." *Warren Buffett*

"If you don't have time to do it right, when will you have the time to do it over?" *John Wooden*

"We are what we repeatedly do. Excellence, then, is not an act, but a habit." *Will Durant*

"Conscientious people … tend to have a lot of satisfaction in their lives because they set tasks and accomplish things." *Leslie Martin*

Do a *completely* good job. Don't make a habit of leaving jobs unfinished. Faltering at the end of a project that you've put a lot of hard work into makes about as much sense as running a race and then stopping just short of the finish line. Go the distance.

Follow through on your commitments. "A thousand words leave not the same deep impression as does a single deed." *Henrik Ibsen*

"If you are faithful in little things, you will be faithful in large ones. But if you are dishonest in little things, you won't be honest with greater responsibilities." *Luke 16:10*

"Essentially, integrity—honesty, virtue and morality—can make or break you in the professional world. And if you choose not to make it a priority, you risk getting stuck with a reputation for deceit." *Tom Popomaronis*

"Choose a good reputation over great riches; being held in high esteem is better than silver or gold." *Proverbs 22:1*

On the Job

"Successful and unsuccessful people do not vary greatly in their abilities. They vary in their desires to reach their potential." *John Maxwell*

"I continue to find my greatest pleasure, and so my reward, in the work that precedes what the world calls success." *Thomas Edison*

"It's fine to celebrate success but it is more important to heed the lessons of failure." *Bill Gates*

"While it's ideal to be closely surrounded by positive, supportive people who want you to succeed, it's also necessary to have your critics. [N]ovices have a preference for positive feedback, but experts want negative feedback, so that they can make progress." *Aimee Groth*

"No man will make a great leader who wants to do it all himself, or to get all the credit for doing it." *Andrew Carnegie*

"Be as enthusiastic about the success of others as you are about your own." *Christian D. Larsen*

"Earn your success based on service to others, not at the expense of others." *H. Jackson Brown Jr.*

"If you can serve others, you get more in return. The more you do that, the more you will get what you want. That's the blueprint to my success." *Bedros Keuilian*

Give more to your coworkers and clients than they expect of you or have asked of you. Try to anticipate what people might need before they ask you for it.

"In everything, treat others as you would want them to treat you. This is the essence of all that is taught in the law and [by] the prophets." *Matthew 7:12*

"Be nice to people on your way up because you'll meet them on your way down." *Wilson Mizner*

When you're preparing to leave a job, organize your desk (and your computer and file cabinets, if applicable). Try to make it as easy as possible for your successor to sort out your business after you've left. Leave behind a good impression of yourself.

Trustworthiness and Integrity

❖ ❖ ❖

"I truly believe that honesty always wins the day. It is said that it takes a hundred lies to hide one act of dishonesty. Therefore honesty surely has to be the best policy." *Trisha Proud*

"Honest people don't hide their deeds." *Emily Brontë (from "Wuthering Heights")*

"If you are faithful in little things, you will be faithful in large ones. But if you are dishonest in little things, you won't be honest with greater responsibilities." *Luke 16:10*

"Essentially, integrity—honesty, virtue and morality—can make or break you in [this] world. And if you choose not to make it a priority, you risk getting stuck with a reputation for deceit." *Tom Popomaronis*

"The reputation of a thousand years may be determined by the conduct of one hour." *Japanese Proverb*

"[I]f I lose mine honour, I lose myself ....,"
William Shakespeare (from "Antony and Cleopatra")

"Whoever walks in integrity walks securely, but whoever takes crooked paths will be found out." *Proverbs 10:9*

Don't rationalize away the impropriety of having an affair with someone when one of you is committed to another person. "You shall not commit adultery." *Exodus 20:14*

"Oh! what a tangled web we weave
When first we practise to deceive!" *Sir Walter Scott*

"Honesty is courageous, dishonesty is cowardly." *Trisha Proud*

In every area of your life, show that you can be trusted.

"Better not to promise at all than to make a promise and not keep it." *Ecclesiastes 5:5*

Don't take or keep anything that you have no right to. "You shall not steal." *Exodus 20:15*

"Each of you must put off falsehood and speak truthfully …." *Ephesians 4:25*

"Live so that when your children think of fairness, caring, and integrity, they think of you." *H. Jackson Brown Jr.*

"This above all: to thine own self be true,
And it must follow, as the night the day,
Thou canst not then be false to any man."
William Shakespeare (from "Hamlet")

Trustworthiness and Integrity

"My meaning simply is,

that whatever I have tried to do in life,
I have tried with all my heart to do well;

that whatever I have devoted myself to,
I have devoted myself to completely;

that in great aims and in small,
I have always been thoroughly in earnest."

Charles Dickens (from "David Copperfield")

Things to Avoid

❖ ❖ ❖

"Test everything. Hold on to what is good and avoid every kind of evil." *1 Thessalonians 5:21-22*

"Have nothing to do with worthless deeds of darkness, but rather expose them." *Ephesians 5:11*

"Do not follow the crowd in doing wrong." *Exodus 23:2*

"So I tell you this, and insist on it in the Lord, that you must no longer live as godless people do, in the futility of their thinking. They are darkened in their understanding and separated from the life of God ...." *Ephesians 4:17-18*

"[S]o much attention is paid to the aggressive sins, such as violence and cruelty and greed with all their tragic effects, that too little attention is paid to the passive sins, such as apathy and laziness, which in the long run can have a more devastating effect." *Eleanor Roosevelt*

Preempt even the smallest sins. Remember that each situation you encounter throughout the day is a little test.

Things to Avoid

Avoid obsessive and excessive behavior. "We should pursue and practice moderation." *Plato*

"Things that cause people to stumble are bound to come, but woe to anyone through whom they come." *Luke 17:1*

"Therefore, let us not pass judgment on one another any longer, but rather decide never to put a stumbling block or hindrance in the way of a brother." *Romans 14:13*

"Be careful ... that the exercise of your rights does not become a stumbling block to the weak." *1 Corinthians 8:9*

Don't use excessive force. "There's no need to buckle on chaps and spurs just to drive the milk cows in." "Don't burn down your house to kill a rat." *Gladiola Montana*

Don't act rashly. "Haste makes waste." *John Ray*

"Do not be in a hurry, but be diligent. Enter into the sublime patience of the Lord." *George MacDonald*

"Never be discouraged because good things get on so slowly here ...." *George MacDonald*

"Don't be impatient for the Lord to act. Keep traveling steadily along his pathway and in due season he will honor you ...." *Psalm 37:34*

"Never think that God's delays are God's denials. Hold on; hold fast; hold out. Patience is genius." *Georges-Louis Leclerc, Comte de Buffon*

"Sensible people will see trouble coming and avoid it ...."
Proverbs 27:12

"I urge you, brothers, to watch out for those who cause divisions and create obstacles contrary to the doctrine that you have been taught; stay away from them." *Romans 16:17*

Beware of those whose benevolent façade is at odds with their malevolent actions. "They come to you in sheep's clothing, but inwardly they are ferocious wolves. By their [actions] you will know them." *Matthew 7:15-16*

Extricate yourself from toxic people. "[D]o not throw your pearls before swine." *Matthew 7:6*

Never reward negative behavior. Don't be an enabler. "This is the hardest of all: to close the open hand out of love and keep modest as a giver." *Friedrich Nietzsche*

Keep away from people who drain your positive energy; don't let anybody suck the life out of you.

Don't allow anybody to rob you of your joy. "Protect your enthusiasm from the negativity and fear of others." *Steve Maraboli*

"Keep away from people who belittle your ambitions. Small people always do that, but the really great make you feel that you too can become great." *Mark Twain*

"Never give up on a dream just because of the length of time it will take to accomplish it." *H. Jackson Brown Jr.*

Things to Avoid

"Do not spoil what you have by desiring what you have not ...." *Epicurus*

"Don't wear yourself out trying to get rich." *Proverbs 23:4*

"Don't chase money. If you are the best in your field, money will find you." *Thomas J. Stanley*

"Do nothing out of selfish ambition or vain conceit." *Philippians 2:3*

Don't cultivate alliances with evil people, regardless of how rich, famous, "important," or popular they are. "Don't be envious of evil men who prosper." *Psalm 37:7*

"Do not be amazed when a man grows rich .... For when he dies, he will take nothing with him ...." *Psalm 49:16-17*

Don't be stingy. "Do not withhold good from those to whom it is due, when it is in your power to do it." *Proverbs 3:27*

"Don't just pray for someone to do something. Be someone who does something. Don't just pray for answers. Be the answer." *L.R. Knost*

"Be careful not to perform your righteous acts before men to be seen by them. If you do, you will have no reward from your Father in heaven. When you give to someone in need, do not announce it like the hypocrites do ... to call attention to their acts of charity." *Matthew 6:1-2*

"Above all, be the heroine of your life, not the victim." *Nora Ephron*

Don't be a whiner, don't pity yourself, and don't try to elicit pity from others.

"Don't get stuck in the potholes of life. Shake off the offenses, shake off what somebody said, shake off self-pity, bitterness." *Joel Osteen*

"To forgive, avoid ruminating on thoughts of being wronged." *Tony Fahkry*

"Life provides losses and heartbreak for all of us—but the greatest tragedy is to have the experience and miss the meaning." "Find the meaning behind whatever it is that you're going through." *Robin Roberts*

"Listen: those who hurt you in the past cannot continue to hurt you now unless you hold on to the pain through resentment. Your past is past! Nothing will change it. You are only hurting yourself with your bitterness. For your own sake, learn from it, and then let it go." *Rick Warren*

"Do not allow the pain of loss to stop the process of living." *Trent Thomas*

"We are products of our past, but we don't have to be prisoners of it." *Rick Warren*

"Don't let yesterday use up too much of today." *Will Rogers*

Things to Avoid

Don't pollute your mind and soul with programs, movies, books, or experiences that have no redeeming value.

"Nor should there be obscenity, foolish talk or coarse joking ...." *Ephesians 5:4*

"Do not let any unwholesome talk come out of your mouths ...." *Ephesians 4:29*

"There is no virtuous necessity for expressing all the dislikes that flash across your feelings. Very often it is necessary as a matter of virtue to spare others the hurt that would be given by freely expressing your opinion." *Lawrence G. Lovasik*

"Get rid of all bitterness, rage and anger, brawling and slander, along with every form of malice." *Ephesians 4:31*

"Make no friendship with a hot-tempered person; do not associate with one easily angered ...." *Proverbs 22:24*

"Stay away from fools, for you won't find knowledge on their lips." *Proverbs 14:7*

"Don't live like ignorant people, but like wise people, making the most of every opportunity ...." *Ephesians 5:15-16*

"Don't wait for good things to happen to you. If you go out and make some good things happen, you will fill the world with hope, you will fill yourself with hope." *Barack Obama*

"Don't be anxious about anything, but in every situation, by prayer and ... with thanksgiving, present your requests to God." *Philippians 4:6*

"When you get into a tight place
and everything goes against you,
till it seems as though you could not hang on
a minute longer,
never give up then,
for that is just the place and time that the tide will turn."
Harriet Beecher Stowe

"Never give up. That's a given. You always fight." *Tiger Woods*

"So one thing I want to say about life is don't be scared and don't hang back, and most of all, don't waste it." *Joan W. Blos*

Love

❖ ❖ ❖

"May the Lord cause you to increase and overflow with love for one another …." *1 Thessalonians 3:12*

"Seek the good in everyone and reveal it, bring it forth." *Rebbe Nachman of Breslov*

"Whoever loves his brother abides in the light,
and in him there is no cause for stumbling." *1 John 2:10*

"Dear children, let's not merely say that we love each other. Let us show the truth by our actions." *1 John 3:18*

"Let no debt remain except the continuing debt to love one another, for whoever loves others has fulfilled the law. The commandments ... are summed up in this one command: 'Love your neighbor as yourself.'" *Romans 13:8-9*

"Not one of you is a believer until he loves for his brother what he loves for himself." *40 Hadith of an-Nawawi 13*

"The main condition for the achievement of love is the overcoming of one's narcissism." *Erich Fromm*

"Why should God reward you if you love only the people who love you?" *Matthew 5:46*

"You have heard that it was said, 'You shall love your neighbor, and hate your enemy.' But I tell you, love your enemies, bless those who curse you, do good to those who hate you, and pray for those who mistreat you and persecute you ...." *Matthew 5:43-44*

"Love keeps no record of wrongs." *1 Corinthians 13:5*

"Whoever would foster love covers over an offense ...." *Proverbs 17:9*

"Above all, love each other deeply, because love covers over a multitude of sins." *1 Peter 4:8*

"The greatest happiness of life is the conviction that we are loved—loved for ourselves, or rather, loved in spite of ourselves." *Victor Hugo*

"Whoever does not love does not know God, because God is love." *1 John 4:8*

"No one is born hating another person because of the color of his skin, or his background, or his religion. People must learn to hate, and if they can learn to hate, they can be taught to love, for love comes more naturally to the human heart than its opposite." *Nelson Mandela*

Friendliness and Friendship

❖ ❖ ❖

"A faithful friend is a sturdy shelter; whoever finds one has found a treasure." *Sirach 6:14*

"Walking with a friend in the dark is better than walking alone in the light." *Helen Keller*

"To be someone's best friend requires a minimum investment of time. More than that, though, it takes emotional energy." *Malcolm Gladwell*

Nurture good friendships; value them like the treasures they are. "The only way to have a friend is to be one." *Ralph Waldo Emerson*

"I've learned many things from Warren [Buffett] over the last 25 years, but maybe the most important thing is what friendship is all about. It's about being the kind of friend you wish you had yourself. Everyone should be lucky enough to have a friend who is as thoughtful and kind as Warren. He goes out of his way to make people feel good about themselves and share his joy about life." *Bill Gates*

Smile. Be approachable. Put people at ease.

"Tell them ... to be peaceful and friendly, and always to show a gentle attitude toward everyone." *Titus 3:2*

If there's a person in your surroundings who is new to the area, do your best to make him or her feel welcome.

"A humble person walks in a friendly world. He or she sees friends everywhere he or she looks, wherever he or she goes, whomever he or she meets. His or her perception goes beyond the shell of appearance and into essence." *Gary Zukav*

"I never met a man I didn't like." *Will Rogers*

"Tolerance is possessing a heart or a spirit that gives room at all times for people's weakness and imperfection with a view to fostering peace and promoting friendship." *John Ibenu*

Acknowledge dates, and make time for events, that are important to your friends. Make reminder notes for yourself so you don't forget about them.

Don't forget to pray for your friends.

"She prayed for every friend and relative in need. Her home was peppered with post-its reminding her who to pray for and why." *Obituary of Betty Puckett Holland*

Friendliness and Friendship

"Accepting someone else's faults, rather than taking them on as a project to be fixed, leaves you the time and emotional energy for enjoying that person." *Gretchen Roberts*

Nobody's perfect. "He who seeks a friend without fault remains without [one]." *Turkish Proverb*

A wise friend knows what to overlook. "Whoever would foster love covers over an offense ...." *Proverbs 17:9*

A brave friend will intervene in your behalf even when the repercussions of doing so are likely to be unpleasant.

A bona fide friend set you straight when you're going off the rails. "Other dogs bite only their enemies, whereas I bite also my friends in order to save them." *Diogenes*

"A gossip tells everything, but a true friend will keep a secret." *Proverbs 11:13*

"Good friends keep on believing in you even when you've stopped believing in yourself." *Origin Unknown*

"I'm a success today because I had a friend who believed in me and I didn't have the heart to let him down." *Abraham Lincoln*

"Friends can help bring out the best in you without expecting perfection. They can remind you not to take life too seriously, as well as give you that much needed boost when you're feeling discouraged." *Amy Morin*

"Focusing on ourselves and wanting our own way will eventually ruin a friendship." *Charles Stanley*

"One who has unreliable friends soon comes to ruin, but there is a friend who sticks closer than a brother." *Proverbs 18:24*

"A friend loves at all times, and is born as a brother for adversity." *Proverbs 17:17*

"In prosperity, our friends know us; in adversity, we know our friends." *John Burton Collins*

Don't let a stupid disagreement alienate you from a good friend.

"We are not enemies, but friends. We must not be enemies. Though passion may have strained, it must not break our bonds of affection." *Abraham Lincoln*

"Do not forsake your friend or a friend of your family." *Proverbs 27:10*

"Greater love has no one than this: to lay down one's life for one's friends." *John 15:13*

Happiness

❖ ❖ ❖

"We are shaped by our thoughts; we become what we think. When the mind is pure, joy follows like a shadow that never leaves." *The Buddha*

"A happy person is not a person in a certain set of circumstances, but rather a person with a certain set of attitudes." *Hugh Downs*

"True happiness is to enjoy the present, without anxious dependence upon the future, not to amuse ourselves with either hopes or fears but to rest satisfied with what we have, which is sufficient, for he that is so wants nothing." *Seneca*

"The foolish man seeks happiness in the distance; the wise [one] grows it under his feet." *James Oppenheim*

"You'll find your happiness lies
Right under your eyes
Back in your own backyard."
*Dave Dreyer, Al Jolson, and Billy Rose
(from "Back in Your Own Backyard")*

"Any man who does not think that what he has is more than ample is an unhappy man, even if he is the master of the whole world." *Epicurus*

"It's not having what you want; it's wanting what you've got." *Jeff Trott (from "Soak Up the Sun")*

"From contentment with little comes happiness." *African Proverb*

"I have learned to seek my happiness by limiting my desires rather than in attempting to satisfy them." *John Stuart Mill*

"As long as there is a lack of the inner discipline that brings calmness of mind, no matter what external facilities or conditions you have, they will never give you the feeling of joy and happiness that you are seeking." *The Dalai Lama*

"A calm and humble life will bring more happiness than the pursuit of success and the constant restlessness that comes with it." *Albert Einstein*

"Happiness doesn't depend on any external conditions, it is governed by our mental attitude." *Dale Carnegie*

"No man is happy unless he believes he is." *Publilius Syrus*

"You are responsible for your own happiness. Too often we're counting on other people to keep us fixed. Someone else to keep us cheered up, encouraged, feeling good about ourselves. You're putting too much pressure on the people in your life. Let them off the hook." *Joel Osteen*

Happiness

"It is only possible to live happily ever after on a day-to-day basis." *Margaret Bonnano*

"For one swallow does not make a summer, nor does one day; and so too one day, or a short time, does not make a man blessed and happy." *Aristotle*

"Joy does not simply happen to us. We have to choose joy and keep choosing it every day." *Jesse Joseph*

"We either make ourselves happy or miserable. The amount of work is the same." *Curlos Castaneda*

"Try to find happiness in everything that is happening around you rather than waiting for good things to happen. You need to work towards happiness. You need to create a happy environment around you ...." *Anurag Aggarwal*

"It all comes to this: the simplest way to be happy is to do good." *Helen Keller*

"Happy are all who search for God and always do his will, rejecting compromise with evil and walking only in his paths." *Psalm 119:2-3*

"The key to living a happy, fulfilling, satisfied life, is really very simple. Just be the person God made you to be, and have the courage to do what God called you to do." *Joel Osteen*

"The person born with a talent they are meant to use will find their greatest happiness in using it." *Goethe*

"If I am only happy for myself, many fewer chances for happiness. If I am happy when good things happen to other people, billions more chances to be happy!" *The Dalai Lama*

"If you want to bring happiness to the whole world, go home and love your family." *St. Teresa of Calcutta*

Gratitude

❖ ❖ ❖

"Cultivate the habit of being grateful for every good thing that comes to you ...." *Ralph Waldo Emerson*

"The more you express gratitude for what you have, the more likely you will have even more to express gratitude for." *Zig Ziglar*

Count your blessings! "Do not spoil what you have by desiring what you have not; remember that what you now have was once among the things only hoped for." *Epicurus*

"We can only be said to be alive in those moments when our hearts are conscious of our treasures." *Thornton Wilder*

"Gratitude is a soil on which joy thrives." *Berthold Auerbach*

"In truth, ... there is nothing which I can esteem more highly than being and appearing grateful. For this one virtue is not only the greatest, but it is also the mother of all of the other virtues." *Cicero*

"Frequently meditate on how good God is to you." *Thomas à Kempis*

"Let all that I am praise the Lord. May I never forget the good things he does for me." *Psalm 103:1-21*

"So I will not be silent; I will sing praise to you. Lord, you are my God; I will give you thanks forever." *Psalm 30:12*

"If you see no reason for giving thanks, the fault lies in yourself." *Tecumseh*

"Take nothing for granted." *Brian Grazer*

If someone loves you, be grateful.

If you have good health, be grateful.

If you have enough to eat, be grateful.

If you can rest when you're tired, be grateful.

If you have a home of some kind, be grateful.

If you aren't a refugee, be grateful.

If war isn't raging in your country, be grateful.

If you live in a free country, be grateful.

If you aren't being persecuted because of your beliefs, be grateful.

Gratitude

"We must find time to stop and thank the people who make a difference in our lives." *John F. Kennedy*

"Let us be grateful to the people who make us happy; they are the charming gardeners who make our souls blossom." *Marcel Proust*

"I thank my God every time I think of you." *Philippians 1:3*

"At times our own light goes out and is rekindled by a spark from another person. Each of us has cause to think with deep gratitude of those who have lighted the flame within us." *Albert Schweitzer*

"A hundred times a day I remind myself that my inner and outer life depend on the labors of other men, living and dead, and that I must exert myself in order to give in the measure as I have received and am still receiving." *Albert Einstein*

"It is beyond one's power to pay back in kind and to the same person each debt of love we owe. But we can pass on to others a service or a kindness wherever we see the need." *Elizabeth Mulligan*

Discerning Truth

❖ ❖ ❖

"Truth does not become more true by virtue of the fact that the entire world agrees with it, nor less so even if the whole world disagrees with it." *Maimonides*

"The time will come when diligent research over long periods will bring to light things which now lie hidden. A single lifetime, even though entirely devoted to the sky, would not be enough for the investigation of so vast a subject.... There will come a time when our descendants will be amazed that we did not know things that are so plain to them." *Seneca*

"To realize that you do not understand is a virtue; not to realize that you do not understand is a defect." *Lao Tzu*

"The best thing you can do for your fellow, next to rousing his conscience, is—not to give him things to think about, but to wake things up that are in him; or say, to make him think things for himself." *George MacDonald*

"The mind is not a vessel to be filled but a fire to be kindled." *Plutarch*

Discerning Truth

"A mind is a terrible thing to waste." *Arthur Fletcher*

"I do not feel obliged to believe that the same God who has endowed us with sense, reason, and intellect has intended us to forgo their use." *Galileo Galilei*

"Men cease to think when they think they know it all." *Horace*

"[T]he unexamined life is not worth living ...." *Socrates*

"In religion and politics people's beliefs and convictions are in almost every case gotten at second-hand, and without examination ...." *Mark Twain*

"[R]e-examine all you have been told in school or church or in any book, and dismiss whatever insults your own soul ...." *Walt Whitman*

"Don't go by gossip and rumor, nor by what's told you by others, nor by what you hear said, nor even by the authority of your traditional teachings." *Anguttara Nikaya*

"Question everything. Take nothing for granted. Don't believe anything because it sounds wise and pious and some holy men said it. See for yourself.... Subject all statements to the actual test of your experience and let the results be your guide to truth." *Bhante Gunaratana*

"You don't need a weather man to know which way the wind blows." *Bob Dylan*

"It is unwise to be too sure of one's own wisdom." *Mahatma Gandhi*

"[I]t is impossible for anyone to begin to learn that which he thinks he already knows." *Epictetus*

"The peculiar evil of silencing the expression of an opinion is that it [robs] ... those who dissent from the opinion, still more than those who hold it. If the opinion is right, they are deprived of the opportunity of exchanging error for truth ...." *John Stuart Mill*

"To make no mistakes is not in the power of man, but from their errors and mistakes the wise and the good learn wisdom for the future." *Plutarch*

"There is nothing to be learned from the second kick of a mule." *Mark Twain*

"Each man makes mistakes, but only a fool persists in his error." *Cicero*

"From the errors of others, a wise man corrects his own." *Publilius Syrus*

"The wise know too well their weakness to assume infallibility; and he who knows most knows best how little he knows." *Thomas Jefferson*

"For knowledge is limited to all we now know and understand, while imagination embraces the entire world, and all there ever will be to know and understand." *Albert Einstein*

Dissention and Anger

❖ ❖ ❖

"A gentle answer turns away wrath, but a harsh one stirs it up." *Proverbs 15:1*

"If you are patient in one moment of anger, you will save a thousand days of sorrow." *Chinese Proverb*

"A patient person has great understanding, but he who is quick-tempered displays foolishness." *Proverbs 14:29*

"Control your temper, for anger abides in the heart of fools." *Ecclesiastes 7:9*

"My dear brothers and sisters, take note of this: Everyone should be quick to listen, slow to speak, and slow to become angry …." *James 1:19*

"Choose your battles wisely." *Sun Tzu*

"I have learned through bitter experience the one supreme lesson: to conserve my anger, and as heat conserved is transmitted into energy, even so our anger controlled can be transmitted into a power …." *Mahatma Gandhi*

"Get rid of all bitterness, rage and anger, brawling and slander, along with every form of malice. Be kind and compassionate to one another, forgiving each other ...." *Ephesians 4:31-32*

"Even here, love, and love alone, frees us. Above all it frees us from the mortal danger of pent-up anger, of that smoldering anger which makes us brood over wrongs we have received." *Pope Francis*

"Any person capable of angering you becomes your master ...." *Epictetus*

"A person's discretion makes him slow to anger, and it is to his credit that he ignores an offense." *Proverbs 19:11*

"Have nothing to do with foolish and stupid arguments ...." *2 Timothy 2:23*

"Part of the happiness of life consists not in fighting battles, but in avoiding them." *Norman Vincent Peale*

"It is an honor for a man to cease from strife." *Proverbs 20:3*

"Remember that a minute of anger denies you sixty seconds of happiness." *H. Jackson Brown Jr.*

"If you become angry, do not let your anger lead you into sin. Do not let the sun go down while you are still angry, and do not give the devil a foothold." *Ephesians 4:26-27*

Dissention and Anger

"Do not make friends with a hot-tempered person; do not associate with one easily angered ...." *Proverbs 22:24*

"As for a person who stirs up division, after warning him once and then twice, have nothing more to do with him ...." *Titus 3:10*

"I appeal to you, brothers, to watch out for those who cause divisions and create obstacles contrary to the doctrine that you have been taught. Stay away from them." *Romans 16:17*

"A person who thinks only about building walls, wherever they may be, and not building bridges, is not Christian." *Pope Francis*

"As for the one who is weak in faith, welcome him, but not to quarrel over opinions." *Romans 14:1*

"Whoever loves an argument loves sin; whoever builds a high gate invites destruction." *Proverbs 17:19*

"Starting a quarrel is like opening a floodgate, so stop before a dispute breaks out." *Proverbs 17:14*

"Do everything without complaining or arguing, so that you may become blameless and pure, children of God without fault in a crooked and perverse generation, in which you shine as lights in the world." *Philippians 2:14-15*

Reaping What You Sow

❖ ❖ ❖

"Do not be deceived; God cannot be mocked. A man reaps what he sows." *Galatians 6:7*

"'Therefore I will judge … each of you according to your actions,' declares the Lord God." *Ezekiel 18:30*

"Let us not become weary of doing good, for in due season we will reap a harvest if we do not give up." *Galatians 6:9*

"Remember this: Whoever sows sparingly will also reap sparingly, and whoever sows generously will also reap generously." *2 Corinthians 9:6*

"Give, and it will be given to you. A good measure, pressed down, shaken together and running over, will be poured into your lap. For with the measure you use, it will be measured to you." *Luke 6:38*

"[T]o you, Lord, belongs lovingkindness, because you reward each person according to what he does." *Psalm 62:12*

Reaping What You Sow

"Everything you do comes back to you." *Origin Unknown*

"We were taught to believe that the Great Spirit sees and hears everything, and that he never forgets; that hereafter he will give every man a spirit-home according to his deserts: if he has been a good man, he will have a good home; if he has been a bad man, he will have a bad home." *Chief Joseph (Nez Perce Tribe)*

Your Judgment Day

❖ ❖ ❖

"Be alert, because you don't know either the day or the hour." *Matthew 25:13*

"Teach us to number our days and recognize how few they are; help us to spend them as we should." *Psalm 90:12*

"Jesus said to them, 'Not everyone who calls out to me, "Lord! Lord!" will enter the Kingdom of Heaven. Only those who actually do the will of my Father in heaven will enter. On judgment day many will say to me "Lord! Lord!" .... But I will reply, 'I never knew you. Get away from me, you who break God's laws.'" *Matthew 7:21-23*

"Who may ascend the mountain of the Lord? Who may stand in his holy place? The one who has clean hands and a pure heart ...." *Psalm 24:3-4*

"Blessed are the pure in heart, for they will see God." *Matthew 5:8*

"It is safe to tell the pure in heart that they shall see God, for only the pure in heart want to." *C.S. Lewis*

Your Judgment Day

"You can be sure that on the Judgment Day everyone will have to give account of every careless word he has ever spoken." *Matthew 12:36*

"The acts of the flesh are obvious: sexual immorality, ... hatred, discord, jealousy, fits of rage, selfish ambition, dissensions, ... and the like. I warn you, as I did before, that those who live like this will have no place in the kingdom of God." *Galatians 5:19-21*

"Truly I tell you, the tax collectors and the prostitutes are entering the kingdom of God ahead of you. For John came to you to show you the way of righteousness, and you did not believe him, but the tax collectors and the prostitutes did." *Matthew 21:31-32*

"The ax is already at the root of the trees, and every tree that does not produce good fruit will be cut down and thrown into the fire." *Matthew 3:10*

"The Lord is slow to anger but … the Lord will not leave the guilty unpunished." *Nahum 1:3*

"We can easily forgive a child who is afraid of the dark; the real tragedy of life is when men are afraid of the light." *Plato*

Fear

❖ ❖ ❖

"Life is either a daring adventure or nothing." *Helen Keller*

"He does not fear bad news or live in dread of what may happen, for he is settled in his mind that God will take care of him." *Psalm 112:7*

"God is our refuge and strength, an ever-present help in trouble. And so we need not fear even if the world blows up and the mountains crumble into the sea …." *Psalm 46:1-2*

"Don't be afraid, for I have ransomed you. I have called you by name; you are mine. When you go through deep waters and great trouble, I will be with you. When you go through rivers of difficulty, you will not drown! When you walk through the fire of oppression, you will not be burned up—the flames will not consume you." *Isaiah 43:1-2*

"Even though I walk through the valley of the shadow of death, I will fear no evil, for you are with me." *Psalm 23:4*

Fear

"Be strong and courageous! Do not fear or tremble before them, for the Lord your God is the one who is going with you. He will not fail you or abandon you." *Deuteronomy 31:6*

"Fear of man will prove to be a snare, but whoever trusts in the Lord is kept safe." *Proverbs 29:25*

"So we say with confidence, 'The Lord is my helper; I will not be afraid. What can mere mortals do to me?'" *Hebrews 13:6*

"Do not be afraid of those who kill the body but cannot kill the soul ...." *Matthew 10:28*

"[E]ven if you should suffer for the sake of righteousness, you are blessed. Do not fear their intimidation, and do not be troubled." *1 Peter 3:14*

"For God has not given us a spirit of fear and timidity, but of power, love, and self-discipline." *2 Timothy 1:7*

"If you want to conquer fear, do not sit home and think about it. Go out and get busy." *Dale Carnegie*

"A great deal of talent is lost to the world for want of a little courage." *Sydney Smith*

"Fortune favors the bold." *Roman Proverb*

"Never let the fear of striking out keep you from playing the game." *Babe Ruth*

"To sin by silence, when they should protest, makes cowards of men." *Ella Wheeler Wilcox*

Be brave enough to stand up for what you believe is right, even if it's at odds with popularly held beliefs.

"The test of courage comes when we are in the minority." *Ralph W. Sockman*

"Courage is not the absence of fear, but rather the judgment that something else is more important than fear." *Ambrose Redmoon*

"The brave man is not he who does not feel afraid, but he who conquers that fear." *Nelson Mandela*

"You gain strength, courage and confidence by every experience in which you really stop to look fear in the face. You are able to say to yourself, 'I have lived through this horror. I can take the next thing that comes along.' You must do the thing you think you cannot do." *Eleanor Roosevelt*

"Courage is resistance to fear, mastery of fear—not absence of fear." *Mark Twain*

"Don't be afraid if things seem difficult in the beginning. That's only the initial impression. The important thing is not to retreat; you have to master yourself." *Olga Korbut*

Worrying

❖ ❖ ❖

Worry less. Pray more.

"You will keep in perfect peace all who trust in you, all whose thoughts are focused on you." *Isaiah 26:3*

"Don't be anxious about anything, but in every situation, by prayer and ... with thanksgiving, present your requests to God. Then you will experience God's peace, which exceeds anything we can understand." *Philippians 4:6-7*

"You must once and for all give up being worried about success and failures. Don't let that concern you. It's your duty to go on working steadily day by day, quite quietly, to be prepared for mistakes, which are inevitable, and for failures." *Anton Chekov*

"Worry is a thin stream of fear trickling through the mind. If encouraged, it cuts a channel into which all other thoughts are drained." *Arthur Somers Roche*

"Worry gives a small thing a big shadow." *Swedish Proverb*

God has it all covered. "Let him have all your worries and cares, for he is always thinking about you and watching everything that concerns you." *1 Peter 5:7*

"God is able to give you more than you need ... for yourselves, and more than enough for every good cause." *2 Corinthians 9:8*

"For this reason I say to you, do not worry about your life, as to what you will eat, or for your body, as to what you will put on. For life is more than food, and the body more than clothing." *Luke 12:22-23*

"Consider how the wild flowers grow. [N]ot even Solomon in all his splendor was dressed as beautifully as they are. And if God cares so wonderfully for flowers that are here today and thrown into the fire tomorrow, he will certainly care for you." *Luke 12:27-28*

Don't waste time fretting about things that you have no control over. "The best thing one can do when it's raining is to let it rain." *Henry Wadsworth Longfellow*

"No amount of guilt can change the past, and no amount of worrying can change the future." *Umar Ibn Al-Khattaab*

"Which of you can add a single hour to your life by worrying about it?" *Matthew 6:27*

"Worry does not empty tomorrow of its sorrow; it empties today of its strength." *Corrie ten Boom*

Sadness and Suffering

❖ ❖ ❖

"Although the world is full of suffering, it is full also of the overcoming of it." *Helen Keller*

"You cannot prevent the birds of sorrow from flying over your head, but you can prevent them from building nests in your hair." *Chinese Proverb*

"Pour out your heart to God, for he is our refuge." *Psalm 62:8*

"In the midst of my utter distress I heard God speak to my heart words of comfort: 'I am a Redeemer. I redeem all things I make all things new. Whatever you've lost I will restore. It doesn't matter what you've done. It doesn't matter what's happened to you. I can take all the hurt, the pain, and the scars. Not only can I heal them, but I can make them count for something.'" *Stormie Ormartian*

"He lifted me out of the pit of despair, out of the mud and the mire. He set me safely on a rock and made me secure." *Psalm 40:1-2*

"Let us not wallow in the valley of despair." *Martin Luther King Jr.*

"Complaining not only ruins everybody else's day, it ruins the complainer's day, too." *Dennis Prager*

"Complaining does not work as a strategy. We all have finite time and energy. Any time we spend whining is unlikely to help us achieve our goals. And it won't make us happier." *Randy Pausch*

"We often add to our pain and suffering by being overly sensitive, over-reacting to minor things, and sometimes taking things too personally." *The Dalai Lama*

"You will continue to suffer if you have an emotional reaction to everything that is said to you. True power is sitting back and observing things with logic. True power is restraint. If words control you that means everyone else can control you." *Warren Buffett*

"Listen: those who hurt you in the past cannot continue to hurt you now unless you hold on to the pain through resentment. Your past is past! Nothing will change it. You are only hurting yourself with your bitterness. For your own sake, learn from it, and then let it go." *Rick Warren*

"There is nothing to be learned from the second kick of a mule." *Mark Twain*

"Each man makes mistakes, but only a fool persists in his error." *Cicero*

Sadness and Suffering

"You can't lie down in the ashes of another person's life."
Mattie Stepanek

"What though the radiance which was once so bright
Be now for ever taken from my sight,
Though nothing can bring back the hour
Of splendour in the grass, of glory in the flower;
We will grieve not, rather find
Strength in what remains behind ...."
William Wordsworth

"Do not allow the pain of loss to stop the process of living."
Trent Thomas

"It's a gift to exist, and with existence comes suffering. There's no escaping that…. So, what do you get from loss? You get awareness of other people's loss, which allows you to connect with that other person, which allows you to love more deeply and to understand what it's like to be a human being …." *Stephen Colbert*

"The pain of grief is just as much a part of life as the joy of love; it is, perhaps, the price we pay for love, the cost of commitment." *Colin Murray Parkes*

"And now I'm glad I didn't know
The way it all would end,
The way it all would go.
Our lives are better left to chance;
I could have missed the pain
But I'd have had to miss the dance." *Garth Brooks*

"Watch, O Lord, with those who wake, or watch or weep tonight ...." *St. Augustine*

"The Lord is near to the brokenhearted and saves those who are crushed in spirit." *Psalm 34:18*

"'I will restore you to health and I will heal you of your wounds,' declares the Lord ...." *Jeremiah 30:17*

"Then your light will break forth like the dawn, and your healing will come quickly ...." *Isaiah 58:8*

"Weeping may endure for a night, but joy comes in the morning." *Psalm 30:5*

"My experiences remind me that it's those black clouds that make the blue skies even more beautiful." *Kelly Clarkson*

"The most beautiful people we have known are those who have known defeat, known suffering, known struggle, known loss, and have found their way out of those depths." *Elisabeth Kübler-Ross*

"You have changed my mourning into dancing ... and clothed me with a garment of joy." *Psalm 30:11*

Challenges and Adversity

❖ ❖ ❖

"Life may bring you to your knees; pray. Then GET UP and participate in the answer." *Steve Maraboli*

"God provides the wind. Man must raise the sail." *St. Augustine*

"Adversity has the effect of eliciting talents which in prosperous circumstances would have lain dormant." *Horace*

"We're going to be better because we grow from what we go through. You can either fall or you can grow. We are determined to grow." *Dallas, Texas SW Div. Police Officer*

"View all problems as challenges: Look upon negatives that arise as opportunities to learn and to grow. Don't run from them ...." *Bhante Gunaratana*

"In the midst of difficulty lies opportunity." *Albert Einstein*

"We are all faced with a series of great opportunities brilliantly disguised as impossible situations." *Charles R. Swindoll*

"Smooth seas do not make skillful sailors." *African Proverb*

"The gem cannot be polished without friction,
nor man perfected without trials." *Chinese Proverb*

"The struggle of life is one of our greatest blessings.
It makes us patient, sensitive, and Godlike." *Helen Keller*

"Life provides losses and heartbreak for all of us—
but the greatest tragedy is to have the experience and
miss the meaning." *Robin Roberts*

"You have to have faith that there is a reason you
go through certain things." *Carol Burnett*

"I definitely think that adversities and challenges are what
make you *you*. I think the Lord challenges us for a reason
and for a purpose[;] once you find that reason and you
find that purpose, that's where you find joy." *Bryce Petty*

"On one hand, we know that everything happens for a
reason, and there are no mistakes or coincidences. On the
other hand, we learn that we can never give up, knowing
that with the right tools and energy, we can reverse any
decree or karma. So, which is it? Let the Light decide, or
never give up? The answer is: both." *Yehuda Berg*

"Never give up. That's a given. You always fight."
Tiger Woods

"Never confuse a single defeat with a final defeat."
F. Scott Fitzgerald

Challenges and Adversity

"After all, you can't learn new things if you cannot admit you're a work in progress. Be open to recognizing your own faults, so you can grow ...." *Ilya Pozin*

"We need more than masking the unpleasant stress responses—we need to learn how to change our behavior and thinking to resolve distressing events in our lives." *Les Ruthven*

"You can suffer the pain of change or suffer remaining the way you are." *Joyce Meyer*

"One of the hardest feelings for the human soul to grapple with is the feeling of being trapped. Trapped in a dead-end job, trapped in an unhealthy relationship, trapped by our own negative habits and inner demons. Even when facing a monumental hardship, if there is a sense of forward movement, of progress, the pain of the hardship is not as intense." *Ani Lipitz*

"The task in front of you is never as great as the Power behind you." *Origin Unknown*

"He gives strength to the weary and increases the power of the weak." *Isaiah 40:29*

"Those who hope in the Lord will renew their strength. They will soar on wings like eagles; they will run and not grow weary; they will walk and not be faint." *Isaiah 40:31*

"In the midst of winter, I found there was, within me, an invincible summer." *Albert Camus*

"The Lord is a shelter for the oppressed, a refuge in times of trouble." *Psalm 9:9*

"The Lord is my shepherd; I have all that I need.
He makes me lie down in green pastures;
He leads me beside quiet waters.
He restores my soul ...." *Psalm 23:1-3*

"Even though I walk through the valley of the shadow of death, I will fear no evil, for You are with me ...." *Psalm 23:4*

"He will command his angels concerning you to guard you in all your ways. They will lift you up in their hands ...." *Psalm 91:11-12*

"The Lord Himself goes before you; He will be with you. He will never leave you or abandon you. Do not be afraid or discouraged." *Deuteronomy 31:8*

"When you go through deep waters and great trouble, I will be with you. When you go through rivers of difficulty, you will not drown. When you walk through the fire of oppression, you will not be burned up—the flames will not consume you." *Isaiah 43:2*

"So we do not lose heart! Though our outer self is wasting away, our inner self is being renewed day by day. For our present troubles are small and won't last very long. They are preparing us for an eternal glory that far outweighs them all." *2 Corinthians 4:16-17*

Challenges and Adversity

"We are pressed on every side by troubles, but we are not crushed. We are frustrated, but not driven to despair. We are persecuted, but never abandoned by God. We get knocked down, but we are not destroyed." *2 Corinthians 4:8-9*

"The rain came down, the streams rose, and the winds blew and beat against that house; yet it did not fall, because it had its foundation on the rock." *Matthew 27:24-25*

"I have put the Lord before me at all times; because he is at my right hand, I will not be shaken." *Psalm 16:8*

"You gain strength, courage and confidence by every experience in which you really stop to look fear in the face. You are able to say to yourself, 'I have lived through this horror. I can take the next thing that comes along.' You must do the thing you think you cannot do." *Eleanor Roosevelt*

"Life is not so much what you accomplish as what you overcome." *Robin Roberts*

"Our greatest glory is not in never falling, but in rising every time we fall." *Confucius*

"You will face setbacks. Some will be larger than others, and sometimes it may even feel like your life is being consumed by one obstacle after another. The key is to maintain a positive attitude and power through; treat every bump in the road as a learning experience ...." *Anjana Bala*

"You must once and for all give up being worried about success and failures. Don't let that concern you. It's your duty to go on working steadily day by day, quite quietly, to be prepared for mistakes, which are inevitable, and for failures." *Anton Chekov*

"If you have made mistakes, even serious ones, there is always another chance for you. What we call failure is not the falling down, but the staying down." *Mary Pickford*

"Failure is just a way for our lives to show us we're moving in the wrong direction, that we should try something different." *Oprah Winfrey*

"When one door closes, another opens; but we often look so long and so regretfully upon the closed door that we do not see the one which has opened for us." *Alexander Graham Bell*

"[E]ach of us, in our journeys through this world, experience our own ... periods of personal destruction, when the sacred spaces within us and within our lives feel razed to the ground, and we feel trapped in the wreckage of what was. But it is precisely during these periods of deepest darkness that the light of compassion shines the strongest in our souls, that the Infinite Itself is revealed before us. Because destruction, like all other forces in the universe, is filled with Divine purpose." *Ani Lipitz*

"My experiences remind me that it's those black clouds that make the blue skies even more beautiful." *Kelly Clarkson*

Challenges and Adversity

"Though the fig tree does not bloom and there are no grapes on the vines, though the olive crop fails and the fields produce no food, ... yet I will rejoice in the Lord; I will be joyful in God my Savior." *Habakkuk 3:17-18*

"In the darkest times of your life, your praise to God should be the loudest. Let the enemy know you're not afraid of the dark." *Stormie Omartian*

"So when you have shut the doors and made a darkness within, remember never to say that you are alone, for you are not alone; God is within, and your Guardian Spirit ...." *Epictetus*

"I will lead the blind down a new path, guiding them along an unfamiliar way. I will brighten the darkness before them and smooth out the road ahead of them. Yes, I will do these things; I will not forsake them." *Isaiah 42:16*

Corrupt Leaders

❖ ❖ ❖

"Isaiah was right when he prophesied about you hypocrites, as it is written: 'These people honor me with their lips, but their hearts are far from me.'" *Mark 7:6*

"Hypocrites! For you are careful to tithe even the tiniest income ... but you ignore the more important aspects of the law: justice, mercy, and faith." *Matthew 23:23*

"Hypocrites! You shut the door of the kingdom of heaven in people's faces. You neither enter yourselves nor let those enter who are trying to go in." *Matthew 23:13*

"You have turned from the way and by your teaching have caused many to stumble." *Malachi 2:8*

"They tie up heavy, cumbersome loads and put them on other people's shoulders, but they themselves are not willing to lift a finger to move them." *Matthew 23:4*

"I appeal to you, brothers, to watch out for those who cause divisions and create obstacles contrary to the doctrine that you have been taught." *Romans 16:17*

Corrupt Leaders

"They have lost all feeling of shame; they give themselves over to vice and do all sorts of indecent things without restraint." *Ephesians 4:19*

"The terror you inspire and the pride of your heart have deceived you, you who live in the clefts of the rocks, who occupy the heights of the hill. Though you build your nest as high as the eagle's, from there I will bring you down,' declares the Lord." *Jeremiah 49:16*

"'As surely as I live,' says the Sovereign Lord, 'you abandoned my flock and left them to be attacked by every wild animal. And though you were my shepherds, you didn't search for my sheep when they were lost. You took care of yourselves and left the sheep to starve.'" *Ezekiel 34:8*

"I now consider these shepherds my enemies, and I will hold them responsible for what has happened to my flock.... I will rescue my flock from their mouths; the sheep will no longer be their prey." *Ezekiel 34:10*

"They come to you in sheep's clothing, but inwardly they are ferocious wolves. By their fruit you will recognize them. Do people pick grapes from thorn bushes, or figs from thistles?" *Matthew 7:15-16*

"Have nothing to do with the fruitless deeds of darkness, but rather expose them." *Ephesians 5:11*

"Resistance to tyrants is obedience to God." *Thomas Jefferson*

Your Relationship with God

❖ ❖ ❖

"I have loved you with an everlasting love." *Jeremiah 31:3*

"God loves each of us as if there were only one of us." *St. Augustine*

You have a direct connection to God. You don't need an intermediary or anybody's permission to speak to Him. No one can stand in the way of Him.

"[N]othing can ever separate us from God's love. Death can't, and life can't. The angels won't, and all the powers of hell itself cannot keep God's love away. Neither the present nor the future, neither the world above nor the world below—nothing will ever be able to separate us from the love of God ...." *Romans 8:38-39*

"You will seek me, and you will find me when you search for me with all your heart." *Jeremiah 29:13*

"God intended that they would seek him and perhaps feel their way toward him and find him. Of course, he is never far from any one of us." *Acts 17:27*

Your Relationship with God

"Pour out your heart to him, for God is our refuge." *Psalm 62:8*

"Because you have made the Lord your defender, the Most High your protector, no evil will overtake you …." *Psalm 91:9-10*

"He reached down from on high and took hold of me; he drew me out of deep waters." *Psalm 18:16*

"He lifted me out of the pit of despair, out of the mud and the mire. He set me safely on a rock and made me secure." *Psalm 40:2*

"We went through fire and flood, but you brought us to a place of great abundance." *Psalm 66:12*

"Those who hope in the Lord will renew their strength.
They will soar on wings like eagles;
They will run and not grow weary;
They will walk and not be faint." *Isaiah 40:31*

"I lift up my eyes to the hills—
Where does my help come from?
My help comes from the Lord,
The maker of heaven and earth....

"The Lord will keep you from all harm—
He will watch over your life;
The Lord will watch over your coming and going
Both now and forevermore." *Psalm 121*

"Don't be impatient for the Lord to act! Keep traveling steadily along his pathway and in due season he will honor you ...." *Psalm 37:34*

"Never think that God's delays are God's denials. Hold on; hold fast; hold out. Patience is genius." *Georges-Louis Leclerc, Comte de Buffon*

"Never be discouraged because good things get on so slowly here …. Do not be in a hurry, but be diligent. Enter into the sublime patience of the Lord." *George MacDonald*

"The Lord Himself goes before you; He will be with you. He will never leave you or abandon you. Do not be afraid or discouraged." *Deuteronomy 31:8*

"The Lord will fight for you; you need only to be still." *Exodus 14:14*

"He will command his angels concerning you to guard you in all your ways. They will lift you up in their hands ...." *Psalm 91:11-12*

"So when you have shut the doors and made a darkness within, remember never to say that you are alone, for you are not alone; God is within, and your Guardian Spirit ...." *Epictetus*

"In the darkest times of your life, your praise to God should be the loudest. Let the enemy know you're not afraid of the dark." *Stormie Omartian*

Your Relationship with God

"So God created mankind in his own image." *Genesis 1:27*

"You created my innermost being. I praise you because I am fearfully and wonderfully made." *Psalm 139:13-14*

God has known you for a long, long time. "Before I formed you in the womb, I knew you …." *Jeremiah 1:5*

God knows you well. He understands you like nobody else understands you.

"You are familiar with all my ways." *Psalm 139:3*

"Even before I speak, you already know what I am going to say." *Psalm 139:4*

"You surround me on every side ..." *Psalm 139:5*

"No eye has seen, no ear has heard, and no mind has imagined what God has prepared for those who love him." *1 Corinthians 2:9*

"You were deliberately planned, specifically gifted, and lovingly positioned on the earth by the Master Craftsman." *Max Lucado*

"'I know the plans I have for you,' declares the Lord, 'plans to prosper you and not to harm you, plans to give you hope and a future.'" *Jeremiah 29:11*

"And what does the Lord require of you? To act justly and to love mercy and to walk humbly with your God." *Micah 6:8*

"I will praise the Lord no matter what happens." *Psalm 34:1*

"Let all that I am praise the Lord. May I never forget the good things he does for me." *Psalm 103:1-21*

"Frequently meditate on how good God is to you." *Thomas à Kempis*

"May his miracles have a deep and permanent effect upon your lives." *Deuteronomy 4:9*

"He surrounds me with lovingkindness and tender mercies. He fills my life with good things!" *Psalm 103:4-5*

"The Lord your God is with you ....
He will take great delight in you;
He will quiet you with his love;
He will rejoice over you with singing." *Zephaniah 3:17*

"The Lord directs the steps of the godly. He delights in every detail of their lives." *Psalm 37:23*

"[H]e is always thinking about you and watching everything that concerns you." *1 Peter 5:7*

"What shall we say about such wonderful things as these? If God is for us, who can ever be against us?" *Romans 8:31*

"So we say with confidence, 'The Lord is my helper; I will not be afraid.'" *Hebrews 13:6*

Your Relationship with God

"Dare to look up to God and say, 'Make use of me for the future as You will.... I refuse nothing which seems good to You. Lead me wherever You want.'" *Epictetus*

"Just as the body without the spirit is dead, so also faith without works is dead." *James 2:26*

"God places us in the world as his fellow workers .... We work with God so that injustice is transfigured into justice, so that there will be more compassion and caring, that there will be more laughter and joy, that there will be more togetherness in God's world." *Desmond Tutu*

"We know that all things work together for the good of those who love God, who are called according to his purpose." *Romans 8:28*

Throughout our lives, God is continually collaborating with us. "I can do all things through Him who strengthens me." *Philippians 4:13*

"Commit everything you do to the Lord. Trust him to help you do it, and he will." *Psalm 37:5*

"By myself I can do nothing .... I seek not to please myself but the One who sent me." *John 5:30*

"[N]ot my will but yours be done." *Luke 22:42*

"Glory belongs to God, whose power is at work within us. By this power he can do infinitely more than we can ask or [even] imagine." *Ephesians 3:20*

"To you, O Lord, I lift up my soul. O my God, in you I trust ...." *Psalm 25:1-2*

"You will keep in perfect peace all who trust in you, all whose thoughts are focused on you." *Isaiah 26:3*

"Trust in the Lord with all your heart, and don't depend on your own understanding. Seek his will in all you do, and he will show you which path to take." *Proverbs 3:5-6*

"Try to find out what pleases the Lord." *Ephesians 5:10*

"You make known to me the path of life; in your presence there is fullness of joy ...." *Psalm 16:11*

"Open my eyes to see wonderful things in your word." *Psalm 119:18*

"Your word is a lamp for my feet, a light on my path." *Psalm 119:105*

"Show me Your ways, O Lord; teach me Your paths. Guide me in your truth and teach me, for you are God my Savior, and my hope is in you all day long." *Psalm 25:4-5*

"I will instruct you and teach you in the way you should go; I will counsel you with my eye upon you." *Psalm 32:8*

"Whether you turn to the right or to the left, you will hear a voice behind you saying, 'This is the way; walk in it.'" *Isaiah 30:21*

Repentance and Redemption

❖ ❖ ❖

"Cast away from yourself all the wrongs you've committed, and make yourself a new heart and a new spirit." *Ezekiel 18:31*

"Create in me a pure heart, O Lord, and renew a right spirit within me. Do not cast me from your presence or take your Holy Spirit from me. Restore to me the joy of your salvation, and grant me a willing spirit to sustain me." *Psalm 51:10-12*

"Your hearts and minds must be made completely new, and you must put on the new self, which is created in God's likeness and reveals itself in the true life that is upright and holy." *Ephesians 4:23-24*

"Whether you and I and a few others will renew the world someday remains to be seen. But within ourselves we must renew it each day …." *Hermann Hesse*

"Whenever night falls, whenever day breaks, search well into your dealings, so will your whole life be one Day of Atonement." *Moses of Evreux*

"There is nothing you've done wrong that is too big for God to fix." *Joyce Meyer*

"Don't you see how wonderfully kind, tolerant, and patient God is with you? Does this mean nothing to you? Can't you see that his kindness is intended to turn you from your sin?" *Romans 2:4*

"The Lord is not slow to fulfill his promise as some count slowness, but is patient ... not wishing that any should perish, but that all should reach repentance." *2 Peter 3:9*

"God doesn't cancel your destiny because you got off course." *Joel Osteen*

"If my people ... will humble themselves and pray and seek my face and turn from their wicked ways, then I will hear from heaven, and I will forgive their sin ....." *2 Chronicles 7:14*

"[E]veryone who calls on the name of the Lord will be saved ...." *Joel 2:32*

"'Come now, let us settle the matter,' says the Lord. 'Though your sins are like scarlet, they shall be as white as snow ....'" *Isaiah 1:18*

"So then, dear friends, since we have these promises, let us purify ourselves from everything that makes body or soul unclean, and let us be completely holy by living in awe of God." *2 Corinthians 7:1*

Repentance and Redemption

"Do not follow the crowd in doing wrong." *Exodus 23:2*

"From now on, then, you must live the rest of your earthly lives controlled by God's will and not by human desires. For you have spent enough time in the past doing what godless people choose to do ...." *1 Peter 4:2-3*

"Do not conform any longer to the pattern of this world, but be transformed by the renewing of your mind." *Romans 12:2*

"Those who live according to the flesh have their outlook shaped by the things of the flesh, but those who live according to the Spirit have their outlook shaped by the things of the Spirit." *Romans 8:5*

"You were taught, with regard to your former way of life, to put off your old self, which is being corrupted by its deceitful desires." *Ephesians 4:23*

"Return all of you who have turned away from the Lord; he will heal you and make you faithful." *Jeremiah 3:22*

"My soul waits in silence for God only; from him is my salvation." *Psalm 92:*1

"I said, 'I will confess my transgressions to the Lord,' and you forgave the guilt of my sin." *Psalm 32:5*

"[T]here is more joy in heaven over one lost sinner who repents and returns to God than over 99 others who are righteous and haven't strayed away!" *Luke 15:7*

"Let us draw near to God with a sincere heart and with the full assurance that faith brings ...." *Hebrews 10:22*

"I now realize how true it is that God does not show favoritism but accepts from every nation the one who fears him and does what is right." *Acts 10:34-35*

"On one occasion an expert in the law stood up to test Jesus. 'Teacher,' he asked, 'what must I do to inherit eternal life?' 'What is written in the Law?' he replied. 'How do you read it?' He answered, 'Love the Lord your God with all your heart and with all your soul and with all your strength and with all your mind, and love your neighbor as yourself.' 'You have answered correctly,' Jesus replied. 'Do this and you will live.'" *Luke 10:25-28*

"Should we offer him thousands of rams and ten thousand rivers of olive oil? Should we sacrifice our firstborn children to pay for our sins? No, O people, the Lord has told you what is good, and this is what he requires of you: to do what is right, to love mercy, and to walk humbly with your God." *Micah 6:7-8*

"I want you to show love, not offer sacrifices." *Hosea 6:6*

"So if you are offering your gift at the altar and there remember that your brother has something against you, leave your gift there before the altar and go. First be reconciled to your brother, and then come back and offer your gift." *Matthew 5:23-24*

Repentance and Redemption

"Go in through the narrow gate. The gate to destruction is wide and the road that leads to it is easy, and there are many who travel it. But the gate to life is narrow and the way that leads to it is hard, and only a few ever find it." *Matthew 7:13-14*

"Fight the good fight for the faith. Take hold of the eternal life that God has called you to ...." *1 Timothy 6:12*

"Repent and turn away from all your bad behavior, so sin won't keep on being a stumbling block for you." *Ezekiel 18:30*

"We do not want you to become lazy, but to imitate those who through faith and patience inherit what has been promised." *Hebrews 6:12*

"Be imitators of God, therefore, as beloved children." *Ephesians 5:1*

"He will take great delight in you; in his love he will ... rejoice over you with singing!" *Zephaniah 3:17*

"You will go out in joy and be led forth in peace. The mountains and hills will burst into song before you, and all the trees of the field will clap their hands." *Isaiah 55:12*

"Surely goodness and mercy will follow me all the days of my life, and I will dwell in the house of the Lord forever." *Psalm 23:6*

The Nature of God

❖ ❖ ❖

"Before you … brought the world into being, you were eternally God, and will be God forever." *Psalm 90:2*

"I am the Lord, the creator of all things. I alone stretched out the heavens. When I made the earth, no one helped me." *Isaiah 44:24*

"Nor is he served by human hands, as if he needed anything, because he himself gives all men life and breath and everything else." *Acts 17:25*

"Before all your people I will do wonders never before done in any nation in all the world. The people you live among will see how awesome is the work that I, the Lord, will do for you." *Exodus 34:10*

"At God's command amazing things happen, wonderful things that we cannot understand." *Job 37:5*

"He has made everything beautiful in its time. [B]ut no one can comprehend what God has done from beginning to end." *Ecclesiastes 3:11*

The Nature of God

"The most important commandment is this: 'Hear, O Israel! The Lord our God is the one and only Lord.'" *Mark 12:29*

"You shall have no other gods before me. You shall not make for yourself an image in the form of anything in heaven above or on the earth beneath or in the waters below. You shall not bow down to them or worship them, for I, the Lord your God, am a jealous God ...." *Exodus 20:3-5*

"Remember the things I have done in the past, for I alone am God! I am God, and there is none like me. Only I can tell you the future before it even happens. Everything I plan will come to pass, for I do whatever I want." *Isaiah 46:9-10*

"Is anything too hard for me?" *Jeremiah 32:27*

"The things which are impossible with men are possible with God." *Luke 18:27*

"'To whom will you compare me? Who is my equal?' asks the Holy One." *Isaiah 40:25*

"No one is good except God alone." *Luke 18:19*

"Don't let anyone call you 'Rabbi,' for you have only one Teacher, and all of you are equal as brothers and sisters. And don't address anyone here on earth as 'Father,' for only God in heaven is your Father." *Matthew 23:9*

"'My thoughts,' says the Lord, 'are not like yours, and my ways are different from yours. As high as the heavens are above the earth, so high are my ways and thoughts above yours.'" *Isaiah 55:8-9*

"When I consider your heavens, the work of your fingers, the moon and the stars, which you have set in place, what is mankind that you are mindful of them, human beings that you care for them?" *Psalm 8:3-4*

"Even though you are so high above, you care for the lowly ...." *Psalm 138:6*

"He knows how many stars there are, and he calls each one of them by name." *Psalm 147:4*

"Not even a single sparrow falls to the ground without your Father knowing it...." *Matthew 10:29*

"God loves each of us as if there were only one of us." *St. Augustine*

He is interested in you. "[H]e is always thinking about you and watching everything that concerns you." *1 Peter 5:7*

"The Lord directs the steps of the godly. He delights in every detail of their lives." *Psalm 37:23*

"I now realize how true it is that God does not show favoritism but welcomes from every nation the one who fears him and does what is right." *Acts 10:34-35*

The Nature of God

God is never unfair. "All his ways are just. A God of faithfulness without injustice, he is righteous and upright." *Deuteronomy 32:4*

"The Lord loves justice and will not forsake his faithful ones." *Psalm 37:28*

"Who of us have not longed for a word from God, … only to feel that he seems absent from the moment? …. Yet later, we realize how very present he was all along." *Charles Swindoll*

"The Lord is close to the brokenhearted and saves those who are crushed in spirit." *Psalm 34:18*

"He heals the brokenhearted and bandages their wounds." *Psalm 147:3*

"He is like a loving father to us, tender and sympathetic …." *Psalm 103:13*

"God blesses those who patiently endure testing and temptation." *James 1:12*

"The Lord's unfailing love and mercy still continue, fresh as the morning, as sure as the sunrise." *Lamentations 3:22*

"He is merciful and tender toward those who don't deserve it; he is slow to get angry and full of kindness and love. He never bears a grudge or remains angry forever." *Psalm 103:8-9*

"The grass withers and the flowers fall,
but the word of our God stands forever." *Isaiah 40:8*

"For I am the Lord; I do not change." *Malachi 3:6*

"God is not man, that he should lie, or a son of man,
that he should change his mind." *Numbers 23:19*

"Every good and perfect gift is from above, and
comes down from the Father of the heavenly lights,
who does not change like shifting shadows." *James 1:17*

* * *

"And the LORD descended in the cloud, stood beside [Moses] there, and called out the name 'Yahweh!' Then the LORD passed over before his face and called out: 'Yahweh! Yahweh God, merciful and gracious, slow to anger, and abundant in kindness and truth ....'" *Exodus 34:5-6*

"Behold, the LORD passed by,
and a great and mighty wind tore into the mountains
and shattered the rocks before the LORD,
but the LORD was not in the wind.
And after the wind came an earthquake,
but the LORD was not in the earthquake.
And after the earthquake came a fire,
but the LORD was not in the fire.
And after the fire there was a sound like a faint whisper."
1 Kings 19:11-12

Asking God for Help

❖ ❖ ❖

"Pour out your heart to God, for he is our refuge." *Psalm 62:8*

"The Lord remains near ... to everyone who calls out to him sincerely." *Psalm 145:18*

"Ask and it will be given to you; seek and you will find; knock and the door will be opened to you. For everyone who asks receives; the one who seeks finds; and to the one who knocks, the door will be opened." *Luke 11:9-10*

"And he told them a parable to the effect that they ought always to pray and not lose heart." *Luke 18:1*

"I've often thought, I'm nobody. Why would God answer my prayer? But God's not impressed by eloquence; he's impressed by our longing for him." *Stormie Omartian*

"Prayer is not asking. It is a longing of the soul." *Mahatma Gandhi*

"Everyone has a different way of connecting to God.... [You simply] must be willing to put forth an effort for your prayer to be answered." *Rabbi Irwin Katsof*

"We do not know what we ought to pray for, but the Spirit himself intercedes for us ...." *Romans 8:26*

"Your Father knows what you need before you ask him." *Matthew 6:8*

"Do not be anxious about anything, but in every situation, by prayer and ... with thanksgiving, present your requests to God." *Philippians 4:6*

"The prayer of a righteous person is powerful and effective." *James 5:16*

"And we are sure of this: that he will listen to us whenever we ask him for anything in line with his will. And if we really know he is listening when we talk to him and make our requests, then we can be sure that he will answer us." *1 John 5:14-15*

"[I]f you sinful people know how to give good gifts to your children, how much more will your heavenly Father give the Holy Spirit to those who ask him!" *Luke 11:13*

"For all prayer is answered. Don't tell God how to answer it." *Edgar Cayce*

"God has three answers to prayer: 'Yes,' 'not yet,' and 'I have something even better in mind.'" *Robin Roberts*

Asking God for Help

"It is better in prayer to have a heart without words than words without a heart." *Mahatma Gandhi*

"When you pray, don't babble on and on as people of other religions do. They think their prayers are answered merely by repeating their words again and again." *Matthew 6:7*

"When you pray, don't be like the hypocrites who love to pray publicly ... where everyone can see them. When you pray, go away by yourself, shut the door behind you, and pray to your Father in private." *Matthew 6:5-6*

"Pray without ceasing." *1 Thessalonians 5:17*

"Keep watching and praying that you may not enter into temptation; the spirit is willing, but the flesh is weak." *Matthew 26:41*

"Search me, God, and know my heart; test me and know my thoughts. See if there is any offensive way in me, and guide me in the everlasting way." *Psalm 139:23-24*

"Create in me a pure heart, O Lord, and renew a right spirit within me. Do not cast me from your presence or take your Holy Spirit from me. Restore to me the joy of your salvation, and grant me a willing spirit to sustain me." *Psalm 51:10-12*

"May the words of my mouth and the meditation of my heart be pleasing in your sight, O Lord, my rock and my redeemer." *Psalm 19:14*

"Prayer is putting oneself in the hands of God, at His disposition, and listening to His voice in the depth of our hearts." *St. Teresa of Calcutta*

"Uphold my steps in your paths, that my feet may not slip." *Psalm 17:5*

"Show me the right path, O Lord; point out the road for me to follow." *Psalm 25:4*

"Send me your light and your truth; may they lead me ...." *Psalm 43:3*

"Guide me in your truth and teach me, for you are God my Savior, and my hope is in you all day long." *Psalm 25:5*

"Open my eyes to see wonderful things in your word." *Psalm 119:18*

"[T]each me good judgment as well as knowledge." *Psalm 119:66*

"God grant me the serenity to accept the things I cannot change; courage to change the things I can; and wisdom to know the difference." *Reinhold Niebuhr*

"Grant me, O Lord, to know what I ought to know, to love what I ought to love, to praise what delights you most, to value what is precious in your sight ...." *Thomas à Kempis*

Asking God for Help

"Lord, make me an instrument of your peace;
Where there is hatred, let me sow love;
Where there is injury, pardon;
Where there is error, truth;
Where there is doubt, faith;
Where there is despair, hope;
Where there is darkness, light;
And where there is sadness, joy.

"O Divine Master,
Grant that I may not so much seek
To be consoled, as to console;
To be understood as to understand;
To be loved as to love." *St. Francis of Assisi*

Made in the USA
Monee, IL
05 September 2019